Invitation

Billy Graham
and the
Lives God Touched

Invitation

Billy Graham
and the
Lives God Touched

Stories of Real People Transformed by God

Basyle and Aram Tchividjian, Grandsons of Billy Graham

Multnomah

INVITATION
PUBLISHED BY MULTNOMAH BOOKS
12265 Oracle Boulevard, Suite 200
Colorado Springs, Colorado 80921
A division of Random House Inc.

Details in some anecdotes and stories have been changed to protect the identities of the persons involved.

ISBN 978-1-60142-149-4

Designed by Kirk DouPonce, DogEared Design
Photos courtesy of the Billy Graham Evangelistic Association
Special thanks to Don Aycock for his editorial assistance on this book.

Published in the United States by WaterBrook Multnomah, an imprint of The Doubleday Publishing Group, a division of Random House Inc., New York.

Printed in the United States of America

"You may be a member of a choir. I don't know who you are or what you are, but you want to give your life to Christ on this opening Sunday afternoon. I'm going to ask you to do a hard thing, because coming to Christ is not easy. So many people have made it too easy. Jesus went to the cross and died in your place. Certainly, you can come a few steps from where you are sitting and stand here, quietly and reverently, and with bowed head. And say, "I need God; I need Christ. I want to be forgiven of my sins. I want a new life, and I want to start a new direction today.""

—BILLY GRAHAM
(Charlotte Crusade, 1958)

DEDICATION

To our grandparents, Daddy Bill and TaiTai, who sacrificed much so many would hear the treasured gospel of Jesus Christ. You lived out love, joy, peace, patience, kindness, goodness, faithfulness, gentleness, and self-control. You showed us what it means to live as authentic Christians. We praise God for your living testimony of His goodness and grace. You have left an eternal impression that continues to draw us to the cross of Christ over and over again.

To the Billy Graham Evangelistic Association and the many people throughout these many years who have served God through their service to this ministry. Through your tireless efforts and countless sacrifices, multitudes from around the globe were able to encounter the living God for the very first time. Your service to our Lord has reaped an eternal harvest.

To all of you who shared your story about God's saving grace through the ministry of Billy Graham. Your stories are the foundation of this book and will introduce many to an eternal relationship with their Lord and Savior. Your experiences are part of God's story and are being used by Him for His honor and glory. Thank you for sharing.

Lastly, and most importantly, we dedicate this book to our ever-loving and gracious Heavenly Father who made the past sixty years possible. We continue to "Declare His glory among the nations, His marvelous works among all the peoples" (Psalm 96:3). God is so very good, and to Him alone be all the glory.

CONTENTS

Invitation

Billy Graham
and the
Lives God Touched

INTRODUCTION

For as long as we can remember, people from all walks of life have approached us and told us about how they came to know Jesus Christ through the work and ministry of Billy Graham. Beyond the magazine covers, best-selling books, White House visits, and Gallup polls are the masses of everyday people who have been forever changed by God through a man we've known simply as "Daddy Bill."

We believe it is now time to share the stories from those who have filled the stadiums, watched televised programs, and read our grandfather's books over the years. A story that needs to be told accompanies every changed life. And Daddy Bill's own story is best told through the accounts of the lives God touched during his many years of ministry. Stories of hope, forgiveness, joy, redemption, and salvation.

Daddy Bill's story began long before we were born. The year was 1934. As the choir sang the famous hymn "Almost Persuaded," a slender sixteen-year-old farm boy sat near the front of the makeshift auditorium struggling with an eternal decision. The words of the hymn lingered in the air...

ANNIVERSARY

HEAR
BILLY GRAHAM
EVERY NIGHT-745

SUMMER BIBLE
SCHOOL
9-A.M. DAILY
LUCILLE VERNON
DIRECTOR
-COME--

Jesus invites you here,
Angels are lingering near,
Prayers rise from hearts so dear;
O wanderer, come!

Young Billy Graham, who had once referred to religion as "hogwash," stood up and made his way to the altar where he surrendered his life to Jesus Christ. This was just the beginning of Daddy Bill's story. Three years later, as a young Bible school student, our grandfather arrived in Palatka, Florida, and was unexpectedly asked to preach his first sermon at Peniel Baptist Church. Though his delivery was impressive, the sermon only lasted eight minutes.

As he practiced preaching to squirrels, rabbits, and palm trees, Daddy Bill thought up excuse after excuse for why he could never become a preacher. But as time passed, the excuses diminished. He knew he couldn't escape the powerful calling of his heavenly Father to preach the Word to all peoples. During these struggles, he was often reminded of God's encouragement to Moses: "Now go; I will help you speak and will teach you what to say" (Exodus 4:12).

The inner battle finally came to an end on a breezy, moonlit Florida evening in March 1938. As Daddy Bill walked the eighteenth green of the Temple Terrace Golf Course, he dropped to his knees. With tears streaming down his face, he cried out, "Oh, God, if You want me to preach, I will serve You."

More than seventy years have passed since that blessed Florida evening, and our grandfather, Billy Graham, has been faithful to that calling. We want you to know that the most important thing—both to us and to Daddy Bill—is the staggering number of lives God has touched through one simple but eternally powerful invitation.

The invitation to meet Jesus Christ.

As grandchildren, we have been blessed to know Daddy Bill in a more intimate and personal way than most people have—after the cameras have been turned off and the crowds have gone home. Here is a man who will get off the phone from speaking with the president of the United States and immediately invite the cook to sit down and join his family for dinner at the kitchen table. Here is a man that would just as soon eat at Morrison's Cafeteria than at the finest restaurant in the world. More comfortable conversing with a cab driver than a president, a CEO, or a movie star, Billy Graham is a man who simply loves people. And it doesn't matter where he is or what he is doing, Daddy Bill has always had time for us, and for that we have been so blessed. We have included stories in this book entitled, "Billy Up Close," about others who have had some type of personal, one-on-one experience with Daddy Bill that made a lifetime impression. We are not surprised.

It is our prayer that in this book you will experience the beauty and sensation of a Billy Graham crusade and more importantly the amazing love and awesome power of the God who has made it all possible. We are so grateful to God for Daddy Bill and are humbled and blessed to call him our grandfather.

—Basyle and Aram Tchividjian

ONE

THAT UNNAMABLE ACHE

"Is there any

"Some of you came tonight, and some are watching on television, asking the same question: 'Is there any hope'?"

—BILLY GRAHAM

Every Billy Graham crusade, every Billy Graham outreach of any kind, begins with the same unnamable ache. That ache is discovered when people from every walk of life come to the end of their resources—finding themselves lost.

There is a pause, a sigh, a groan and they look up from an empty bottle of pills, or they step outside and begin a listless ramble along the highway, or they come trembling to the brink of suicide. And at that moment—at just the right moment—a message comes to them.

hope?"

Perhaps they scan a few words from a crumpled booklet in the half light of an airplane reading lamp, or they hear a clear voice ringing out from the car radio, or they see the flickering image of a man at a podium in a sea of people on the television. And somehow that message breaks through to their deepest need and speaks straight to the ache with words from God on the lips or from the pen of Billy Graham.

The ache—that sense of emptiness, of having no purpose—is where many of our stories begin. Millions of people ached. And Billy Graham—arms outstretched, eyes brimming with compassion— gave them an invitation.

A REMEDY FOR THE ACHE

TRICIA, FROM SOUTHERN CALIFORNIA, felt the ache. Actually, she felt it twice. The first time she was only sixteen, pregnant, and strung-out on drugs. Tricia was hurting deep within—in heart and body. She wandered into a tent set up on the beach and listened to Billy Graham speak about things she

Millions of people ached. And Billy Graham— arms outstretched, eyes brimming with compassion— gave them an invitation.

had never heard of before, about truths she had never dared imagine—unconditional acceptance, a free gift of peace with God, a new life. There was something here! Something true. Something for her.

Minutes later, Tricia found herself at the altar, kneeling awkwardly in the sand. She describes the moment: "I gave my life to Christ. A former prostitute with mascara running down her tear-streaked cheeks counseled me. I left wondering what had just happened."

What had happened? There, face-to-face with a woman she had never met, Tricia gave the life she had never wanted to the God she had always needed. She will never forget those mascara streaks, the gentle burn of sand beneath her knees, the crescendo of waves crashing just outside with the voices of

There, face-to-face with a woman she had never met, she gave the life she had never wanted to the God she had always needed.

hundreds praying, and the feeling of good news washing over her—at last, something for the ache!

But as real and powerful as that moment was, Tricia soon found herself caught up in a struggle with her old ways. "There was always that still small voice in my deepest parts," she writes, "but I tried to bury it in rebellious living. I was successful almost to the point of death, deep despair and heartache driving me to the very edge of suicide. I think God was saying, 'Your mouth says no—no, but your heart is saying yes—yes.' And it was true, because that ever-present, never-ending love of God finally captured me."

It's as if that same invitation echoed in her soul. After several stops and starts, Tricia's life was finally filled with purpose and hope. She surrendered her life to Christ and discovered the remedy for her deepest need. What stands out in Tricia's memory of her journey is that humble starting place: "It all began in a tent on a beach forty years ago, when I listened to a man named Billy Graham!"

A WONDERFUL KIND OF SEED

TRICIA'S STORY IS NOT UNCOMMON. The remainder of this book is filled with stories very much like it. An invitation goes out. Regardless of life's circumstances, people hear it and answer, "Yes—yes." The whole thing may seem a little ordinary. But what we miss is that the invitation is a kind of seed. A very powerful and wonderful kind of seed. Once sown, it replants a life. The result is a beautiful harvest that yields eternal fruit.

The invitation is a very powerful and wonderful kind of seed.
Once sown, it replants a life.

We hope to help you see Billy Graham as he really is. A farm boy from North Carolina who had but one crop to sow, one kind of seed. Up and down the length of this great United States and across oceans abroad, he sowed the seed of the gospel to the aching, to throngs of ordinary, life-worn people.

Viewed this way, these humble stories as the true record of a harvest on a scale never before seen. For whether in person or by book, radio, television, or film, Billy Graham has been able to proclaim God's invitation to more than 2 billion people in 185 countries.

"GOD HELP ME"

JUST GETTING THERE, though, getting to that invitation, is often the problem. But sometimes running away brings people to the very thing they were longing for.

One night Sandra from Wisconsin decided to leave everything behind. After a day of drinking and arguing with her husband, Sandra went out to the road and started walking.

No one came after her. As she paced alongside the highway, Sandra took an inventory of her disappointing life thus far: Family, friends, and acquaintances had all let her down. She had let herself down. Most devastating, though, was the belief that God had abandoned her. Her life was a mess, a bottomless pit of sadness and despair.

She was walking away from the pain because it hurt so badly. But then something extraordinary happened. "As I was walking," Sandra explains, "I remember looking up at the stars, and in my half stupor, I said, 'God, help me.' Those three words saved my life."

A couple of people she didn't know picked Sandra up and dropped her off at a restaurant, and she eventually made it back home. But the gloom—that dark swirling void that seemed to swallow her—simply got worse. "I was feeling really bad about myself and concluded that my husband and children would be better off without me, so I decided to leave them. I got some friends to take me to a bus station, and I purchased a ticket to Las Vegas. At this point, no one knew where I was."

No one, perhaps, except God.

Sandra got off the bus in Salt Lake City and encountered a woman named Nancy handing out pieces of paper. She stopped and asked about them. The woman explained that she was representing the Billy Graham Evangelistic Association and was simply telling people about Jesus.

She stood on that noisy street corner listening to the woman tell
her about Jesus, hanging on to every word for hope.

Jesus? Sandra wondered. *I grew up in church. What does Jesus have to do with this? Besides*, she thought, *I know everything there is to know about Jesus.*

But for the next two hours time stopped for Sandra. She stood on that noisy street corner listening to the woman tell her about Jesus, hanging on to every word for hope. As Sandra left, her new friend gave her a New Testament and some of Billy Graham's books. Sandra treasured that New Testament and began to read it for herself.

The seed that had been planted on the streets of Salt Lake City was about to blossom in ways Sandra never could've imagined. Sandra describes her transformation: "In the front part of the Bible, Billy Graham had inserted a page called 'How to Become a Christian.' He had written out the four spiritual laws. I read them and then came to the Sinner's Prayer":

Dear Lord Jesus, I know that I am a sinner and need Your forgiveness.

I believe that You died for my sins. I want to turn from my sins.

I now invite You to come into my heart and life.

I want to trust and follow You as Lord and Savior.

In Jesus's name, amen.

"I read through it and thought, *What does that mean?*" Sandra says. "So I read it again, and all of a sudden the light came on. *Oh, that's what it means!*" Sandra's life was never the same.

Drawn as it is from Scripture, the Sinner's Prayer has a simple power. Embracing the words for yourself is an amazing experience. In a few sentences you come to know yourself as never before, and you come to know God as you never imagined Him to be.

Sandra describes what happened next. "My living room came alive with the presence of the Lord. He was so real. What was happening to me was so real. I could feel the burden of sin being lifted from me, and my whole being was changed in an instant. I will always have that sweet woman, Nancy, to thank for taking the time to talk to me. My salvation was sealed on June 25, 1972."

As she looked for something to fill the bottomless pit, Sandra took herself on a long journey that eventually led her to the cross of Christ and to peace with God. The seed had taken root and was beginning to grow.

A KNOT AT THE END OF THE ROPE

THE ROAR OF NIAGARA FALLS was not enough to drown out the question raging in Carolyn's mind: *Is life worth living?* The answer seemed evident because of the very fact that she was here. She had not come to sightsee.

She sat in her car, working up the courage to throw herself over the falls. It seemed like the only answer for Carolyn. There was a kind of hope in simply being at the end of her rope.

But Carolyn didn't realize there was a knot at the end of her rope, one that would keep her from jumping over the edge. That knot was a book filled with stories of people whose lives had been dramatically changed by God at a Billy Graham crusade.

What a strange irony! To read about glimpses of hope on the brink of the cliff. Carolyn's fingers trembled as she tried to hold the book steady enough to see if anything in it could pull her off her deadly course.

Carolyn caught a glimmer of hope— many of the stories began just like hers but ended far differently.

As she began to read, something wonderful happened. Carolyn caught a glimmer of hope— many of the stories began just like hers but ended far differently. Listen: "As I read the testimonies, I thought that maybe Jesus could change my life. I could always come back next week and jump. I also had a tract and prayed the prayer on the back and asked Jesus to forgive my sins. God changed my life that day."

The ending had been rewritten! A message came...an invitation. The ache was answered. Carolyn has no explanation for why she is still alive other than the fact that God brought her to Himself that day many years ago at the edge of Niagara Falls. And while Billy Graham has never met Carolyn, he would no doubt be gratified to know that God's message continues to rewrite stories. And that those stories, often coming out of very dark places, are now filled with light and hope, a hope that is embodied in the gospel as preached by Billy Graham.

Countless people have discovered that when they begin to reach out to God, He has already been reaching out to them.

A GOD-SHAPED VACUUM

NOT ALL SENSES OF NEED ARE CAUSED by bad actions. Millions feel, as a philosopher once put it, that there is a "God-shaped vacuum" in their heart. They know that something big is missing from their lives and that something is gnawing at them, prompting them to search for some way to feed that hunger. Many begin searching early in life for the missing piece and ultimately discover that it is actually a relationship. A relationship with God.

Stephan grew up in the idyllic mountains of Switzerland. He was surrounded by a loving family yet found himself yearning for something he could not name. "As I reached my early teens," he says, "I grew restless in my heart, not knowing why. I had all the world could possibly offer and yet no peace, no contentment, no joy." He searched, looking to family and even his church to give him that elusive peace. "Gradually I realized that my need was spiritual."

But Stephan grew weary with the search. "With quiet desperation, I pursued answers on my own but could never seem to hold the truth in my hand—as a handful of sand, it always seemed to slip through my fingers, leaving me frustrated and discouraged. And there was no one to help, nowhere to turn."

Or so he thought.

"With quiet desperation, I pursued answers on my own but could never seem to hold the truth in my hand."

One day Stephan's father gathered the family and shared that he had established a personal relationship with God. At first no one understood. The family attended church; they were good people. Of course, they knew about God. But Stephan's father described a book he had been reading called *Peace with God,* written by an American evangelist named Billy Graham. The family could see the tremendous change in the father, so young Stephan asked to borrow the book.

As Stephan read, the words seem to lift off the page and blow across the cold embers of his heart. Soon those embers became a living fire that seared away the sense of emptiness he had known. He had found what the title promised—peace with God.

Stephan spoke of that experience as if talking directly to the book's author: "You gave me the words that would forever quench the thirst in my soul. You told me how to be born again according to the Scriptures. That night, a fifteen-year-old knelt by his bed, alone with God, and invited his Savior, Jesus Christ, to forgive his sins and live forever in his heart. Peace finally filled my soul."

Stephan had no way of knowing at that time how radically his life would change. Years later he had the privilege of getting to know the American

evangelist that had changed his life. In fact, Stephan Tchividjian married one of Billy Graham's daughters and became the father of the authors of this book!

Stephan concludes, "Thank you, Billy Graham. You have been a father to me and the grandfather to my children and a friend who is and forever will be closer than a brother. But above all, you introduced me to our God and showed me what it means to honor Him and walk with Him."

Every person has that God-shaped vacuum. Some discover early in life that God longs to fill that space and invite Him in. Others flail around for years, getting nowhere but deeper into loneliness and despair. But the ultimate answer for life's most central needs are found in the gospel Billy Graham has spent a lifetime sharing: "God loves you and wants to have a relationship with you."

"YES, THERE IS HOPE!"

SELDOM DO TWO PEOPLE START OUT on exactly the same paths in life. The most important thing, however, is not the starting place but the finish line. Though the people who share their stories in this book have their own personal experiences, all have moved forward to find purpose and hope in this life and in the life to come

Many began with an ache that seemed to have no name. Was it loneliness? Despair? Worthlessness? Whatever the name or the cause, these people experienced what countless others have discovered as well. That ache has only one lasting remedy—the embracing love of God in Jesus Christ.

Billy Graham has devoted his life sowing the seeds of this precious message called the gospel. No one will ever know the personal sacrifices he endured so that others—millions of others—would hear of God's amazing love. Billy Graham has been able to invite these seekers to find the answer to the most important question they have ever asked—"Is there any hope?"

The answer is "Yes, there is hope!"

Billy Up Close

I once heard a pastor speak years ago at my church. He had attended a seminar for ministers, pastors, and other church leaders. During the service in this huge auditorium, there was a time when they knelt at their seats and spent time in prayer. He could not help but listen to the distinct voice behind him; it sounded familiar, but he just couldn't place it. The man was weeping uncontrollably and crying out to God. "Please Father, forgive me of my sins. I am nothing! Forgive me of my failure, and help me become the man of God You want me to be!" This went on and on and the minister couldn't wait to stand and take a quick glance behind him to see who this man was. As the prayer time ended, the minister began to stand and noticed that the person seated behind him was the great Billy Graham. As I listened to this man speak about his experience, he began to cry, saying over and over how humbled he was to hear such a great man of God speak those words and how as a pastor it truly impacted him and changed his life.

—Bradley from Texas

TWO

TWO WORDS

TWO WORDS

"There may never be a moment

"You have tried everything and failed many times. You can come just as you are. You can come to Christ right now—wherever you are and just as you are—and the angels of heaven will rejoice!"

—BILLY GRAHAM

"Puff Graham." Two words that changed history. William Randolph Hearst, owner of the *Los Angeles Examiner* and *Los Angeles Herald Express,* sent out a telegram with those two words to his newspaper editors. And those words set off a chain of events that is still reverberating throughout earth and eternity. In the summer of 1949, Hearst told his reporters to publicize the meetings being held in a tent in Los Angeles. The speaker was a young fellow named Billy Graham.

Many heard the buzz and came. Slowly at first, but momentum built toward the final night, when 11,000 people

quite like this for you."

squeezed into a tent at the corner of Washington and Hill while thousands of others milled about the area unable to get in. What had been scheduled as a three-week event turned into an eight-week crusade.

Two words. But these were not the only two words that would turn people's lives around. Graham himself would utter others—pleas, commands, prayers.

"Come today."

"Don't hesitate."

"God loves."

"God forgives."

"Accept Christ."

THAT VOICE

THAT SUMMER, IN 1949, Jean was living in Los Angeles, and her mother was in town visiting. They had read newspaper articles about the lanky preacher everyone seemed to be talking

A NEW EVANGELIST ARISES

BILLY GRAHAM HOLDS A REVIVAL IN LOS ANGELES AND CONVERTS 6,000 OF HIS 300,000 LISTENERS

Now, as then, Graham's invitation to that relationship has remained simple and focused: "Come today."

about, the guy with the "voice of a trumpet" and the "courage of a lion." Could anyone actually be that good? Was this for real or just another Hollywood sideshow?

Jean and her mother decided to find out for themselves. They paid their nickel fare and boarded the streetcar one evening, heading for the corner of Washington and Hill.

Getting seats in those early days wasn't a problem. But seats would be harder to come by after more press coverage. "The crowd was not as large as it later became, but the tent was packed," Jean said. The two women could feel the electricity in the air as the service began. The blazing lights. The worship-filled music. And then the young man with that voice. That distinctive voice Jean will never forget.

Perhaps it was her curiosity, piqued by the hype in the news, that brought Jean and others like her from all across the city to the crusade that night. Perhaps it was something more. Years later, Jean still clearly remembers being part of history—witnessing the beginning of a ministry that would span more than fifty years and impact the lives of millions. Jean has always felt a special bond with Billy Graham, the young man who captivated her with the message of God's love. She remains humbled to have been among those listening at one of his first crusades.

Now, as then, Graham's invitation to that relationship with Christ has remained simple and focused: "Come today." And countless numbers have responded—and have discovered the relationship that some longed for, others resisted, but all received.

Don, for example, attended a crusade without even knowing why he went.

PERFECT TIMING

AS DON WAS LEAVING WORK one day, he heard on the radio that Billy Graham would be speaking at a stadium in San Jose that evening. Don wasn't sure why, but he wanted to hear Graham. "Something prodded me to go, but I thought, *No way will I be able to get tickets or parking. I figured I'd drive by anyway.*" As Don steered his car toward the parking area for the stadium, he noticed something surprising. "Right in front of the stadium was a parking spot—waiting for me. So I parked and walked up to an entrance. As I approached, I saw security and thought, *This will be the end of this.* To my surprise, they waved me inside."

So far, so good. Don now expected that he'd end up in the nosebleed section, so far away that he'd barely be able to see or hear the famous evangelist. Again he was surprised. "A man waved me down the aisle to a door and down some stairs to a seat that was directly across from Billy Graham. I was stunned." Don settled into the amazing seat and began to listen— really listen. Billy Graham spoke about life and the possibility of having a real relationship with God. Then, as he always did, Graham invited people who wanted that relationship to come forward and learn more.

Don found himself among the group who came forward that evening. "I felt as if someone had picked me up, and I walked right up to the front of the stage and looked at Billy and said, 'I will.'" That night Don found the relationship Graham had promised and he knew that his life would never be the same. Don, like countless others, wandered into a Billy Graham crusade out of curiosity and walked out as a new person.

Billy Graham has always been quick to embrace new means of communicating the gospel. He began with face-to-face crusades but soon expanded to radio, television, books, and movies. Theresa was just one person touched by God's healing power through television.

Don, like countless others, wandered into a Billy Graham crusade out of curiosity and walked out as a new person.

THERESA WAS DEEPLY TROUBLED as a child. Something had gone terribly wrong. At the tender age of five, Theresa reached an incredible conclusion. "I decided that I wanted to die."

But what could a child know of such things? Sadly, she knew enough. Theresa had a clear image of how the task would be accomplished. "I remember standing in the dark kitchen with a knife to my heart, thinking how painful it might be but how quickly all my suffering could end. My young mind seemed so full of grownup anger and hurt."

By age five, Theresa had seen more than any child should. "I had a loving mom, who chose to leave my abusive father and struggle to care for me and my younger sister all alone." Theresa's tender young mind could not comprehend the torture she had witnessed before her mother left the abusive relationship, and it pushed her to the edge of madness.

At the age of six, Theresa was hospitalized for mental illness. "The doctors told my mom it was the

"That night…Billy Graham…brought the warmth of the Lord right where I was, and at the age of six, I gave my life to the Lord."

best place for me considering the circumstances… So there I sat—alone, sad, and depressed in a dreary, uncaring, and cruel place."

One evening the other children in the ward had asked to watch a popular television program. As the nurse was changing channels, Theresa noticed that a Billy Graham crusade was on. The images on the screen immediately brought back some of the few happy memories from Theresa's past. "When a Billy Graham crusade would air, my Mom, my sister, and I would sit in front of the television and listen to every word."

Theresa pleaded with the nurse to turn the channel back to Billy Graham. "The other kids begged her not to, but I refused to give up. That night I watched Billy Graham from that cold and lonely place. He brought the warmth of the Lord right where I was, and at the age of six, I gave my life to the Lord."

It was a life-altering evening. "I wept as I sat in front of that television set. My little heart ached, and the more I cried, the more I was comforted by the words spoken by this great man. My life changed that night."

The words about God's love formed the key that unlocked the grip of fear and bitterness that had imprisoned Theresa's young heart. And everyone noticed the change. Just a few days later, Theresa's mother took her home. "I never contemplated suicide again."

Many people, like young Theresa, aren't able to articulate what they need. They only know they have an empty spot in their heart that cries out for healing. Others know exactly what the vacant places in their hearts are yearning for and will expend whatever time and effort necessary to get it. Alexander was such a person.

ACROSS THE CONTINENTS

IN 1969, ALEXANDER WAS A TEENAGE young man growing up on a remote farm in the Australian outback. On Sunday evenings, while the rest of his family watched television, Alexander would climb into the cab of his small truck and tune in to *The Hour of Decision* on the radio and listen to Billy Graham speak about things that touched the deepest longings of Alexander's soul. One evening the announcer said something that really caught his attention. Billy Graham was coming to Australia!

"When I heard about the Melbourne crusade, I quickly made plans to attend." After scraping together part of his farm allowance, Alexander traveled the 350 kilometers to Melbourne with a friend from his tiny bush church. He sat with his friend, the only other person he knew in that crowd of thousands, soaking up every word. Given his rural background, Alexander found the experience nearly overwhelming. The huge crowd. The large choir. The opportunity to finally see the man whose voice he had listened to on so many Sunday nights.

"When Billy extended the invitation to accept Christ, I went forward along with many others. But I wasn't left standing for long. Soon a volunteer counselor approached and guided me through helpful literature about giving my life to Christ. It was an unforgettable experience. That counselor kept in touch with me after my return to the farm and guided me on my new walk with Christ."

Nearly four decades later, Alexander remains on the path on which God placed him in 1969. Though still living in a remote area in Australia, Alexander has a few more resources today, including the Internet and information from many avenues. But even after all the time that has passed, his memory of the Melbourne crusade hasn't diminished. "I will always be grateful for Billy Graham's unique preaching style and his total commitment to God."

Alexander found what he had been searching for. Others, like Donna, were blessed to discover far more than they thought they needed.

COMING FROM THE CHOIR

DONNA WAS A FAN OF THE ANGELS—the Los Angeles Angels baseball team. When she was fifteen, she and her church choir were asked to be part of a larger choir singing at the Billy Graham crusade in Anaheim. It was being held at the stadium where the Angels played, so Donna said yes. She admits that she was more excited about being in her beloved team's stadium than about hearing Dr. Graham speak.

But that would change once the service began.

"I had never fully understood God's love for me," Donna says. "That night I did! A rush of emotion, the feeling of pure safety and overwhelming love, came over me. I started to cry as the words of the beautiful songs we had been practicing for weeks began to sink in. What each word was doing to my heart—it was as if a two-thousand-pound weight was lifted off my chest. Relief and peace washed over me as God took control."

Donna's experience captures precisely what Graham has always desired for his life and ministry.

"Billy Graham's message was the catalyst for my walk with Christ. He opened my eyes to the light when I couldn't even see that I was in the dark."

Donna hadn't even realized she was in the dark when God opened her eyes at Angel Stadium. Linda, on the other hand, knew she was stumbling in darkness but doubted that God would ever light her path.

"It was as if a two-thousand-pound weight was lifted off my chest. Relief and peace washed over me as God took control."

AN UNEXPECTED RESPONSE

OFTENTIMES WHEN PEOPLE call out to God from life's deepest valleys, they don't honestly expect a response. Linda was familiar with that feeling. Although she grew up in a Christian home, Linda had drifted away from God during her teenage years and had become totally immersed in what the world had to offer.

"After two marriages and two children, I could no longer ignore the vacant spot in my heart. I started attending church and reading the Bible, but I was hesitant to totally commit myself to Christ. 'If Billy Graham comes to this area again,' I promised God, 'I will go and give myself to You.' I thought this would never happen since Dr. Graham rarely made crusade appearances."

Little did Linda know, God would respond to her call in an amazing way. "Soon after making this promise, I was shocked to read in the paper that Dr. Graham was going to be at Qualcomm Stadium in San Diego! I never could've predicted that my promise to God would be tested. On Mother's Day 2003, my son and I attended the San Diego crusade, where I came forward for my Lord, Jesus Christ."

The vacant spot in Linda's heart is now filled as a result of God's unexpected response to Linda's call.

Unexpected. That describes the way God often encounters people like Linda. It also defines the experience of Naomi.

A Billy Graham crusade was being televised, and like millions of others, Naomi was about to discover relief for the numbness that characterized her life.

NAOMI HAD BEEN ZIPPING THROUGH LIFE, gathering momentum but going nowhere. She knew something was wrong. At first she couldn't put a finger on the problem—a numbness within that she couldn't quite reach. What was going on? Did other people feel like this too? What did they do about it?

In 1976, Naomi had just moved to Wyoming with a new baby but no husband. "I was lost and alone, and it was Christmas Eve. My friend and her parents wanted me to go to a Christmas Eve service, but I told them I'd rather stay home." Soon after everyone left, Naomi found herself pacing back and forth in front of the television, not really paying attention to what was on.

As she paced, the sound of singing coming from the television caught Naomi's attention. She lurched to a standstill midstep. A Billy Graham crusade was being televised, and like millions of others, Naomi was about to discover relief for the numbness that characterized her life.

"I stopped and listened as the choir sang. My hardened heart seemed to soften a little. I was tired, so I put my baby in the crib in the next room and went back to finish watching the crusade. I hardly remember what was said, but as I walked into my bedroom later, I felt as though God was there. The only place His presence couldn't be felt was inside me. Inside I felt a void, an emptiness I couldn't describe."

Pointing to her heart, a gesture that no one but God could see, Naomi acknowledged His presence in the room. "Whatever is out there?" she said. "I want it in here." She laid her hand over her heart. "Immediately God filled me with His Spirit, and I felt peace."

Many years later, that God-given serenity is still with Naomi. "To this day, I attribute my salvation directly to the ministry of Billy Graham. God's presence in the crusade that Christmas Eve stopped me dead in my tracks." Because of that unexpected moment, Naomi's life was pointed in a new direction.

And Naomi received what God freely offers—forgiveness, love, and peace.

COME JUST AS YOU ARE

MANY PEOPLE CAN REMEMBER the first time they heard the voice of Billy Graham. Perhaps it was at a crusade, on television, through a radio, or on the pages of one of his books. Often the message seemed like an accident or an interruption. But wherever his voice is heard, the invitation is always the same: *Come just as you are. You don't need to do anything before opening your heart to receive Christ. The work has already been done.*

Yes, those two words—"Puff Graham"—changed history. They lifted an obscure preacher from a dairy farm in North Carolina and set him on center stage in a global drama that has lasted more than half a century. And those words have resulted in millions responding to the invitation to "come just as you are."

Billy Up Close

It was 1987 and I was serving my first year as youth pastor at Calvary Baptist Church in Burbank, California. The position was interesting because Calvary Baptist didn't actually have any youth. Our "youth group" was made up of unchurched teens from local neighborhoods, none of whom had professed Christ.

One day I received a call from a woman at Billy Graham's World Wide Pictures regarding an advanced screening for their new movie, *Caught.* They were holding the screening at Universal Studios, and she wanted to know if I would bring my youth group. They especially wanted reactions from non-Christians and asked me to encourage my Christian youth group to bring their non-Christian friends. I'm sure she was surprised to hear that we didn't actually have any Christians in our group.

The night of the screening was a hoot. My friend Martin and I took eight teen boys. Other youth groups were arriving by bus, dressed nicely for the occasion and walking quietly and politely to the theater. Our guys were all over the place. They were underdressed, loud, and obnoxious, and were running everywhere while checking out Universal Studios after hours. We stuck out like sore thumbs in an elegant hand gallery.

After we finally gathered them (and got them to put out their cigarettes), we made our way into the theater. It was a first-class theater with high-backed reclining chairs. Our guys naturally pushed their way to the front of the theater where they proudly sat down front and center, in full view of everybody.

One of our boys asked where the water fountain was. Since we finally had them corralled and sitting down, I told him I'd go find one. I walked up to an official-looking man at the back of the theater and asked where we could find a water fountain. This man turned out to be Bill Brown, the president of World Wide Pictures at the time. He asked my name and said, "I'd like you to meet someone." Then he tapped the shoulder of a tall man with his back to us. "Billy, I'd like you to meet Ray."

The tall man turned around. Sure enough, it was Billy Graham. I had no idea he would be there that night and was completely caught off guard. I think I managed to squeak out something brilliant like, "Hello. Nice to meet you. I've heard you speak."

Dr. Graham shook my hand, smiled, and with a twinkle in his eye nodded toward the front of the theater. "Are those your boys?" he asked. I looked up and saw Martin doing his best to contain eight overly exuberant boys, who were rocking all the way back in their chairs as fast as they could go. They looked like eight alternating levers in some wildly gyrating machine.

"Excuse me," I said, racing to the front of the theater. We finally got the boys settled down in time for the movie. I got the clear impression that Dr. Graham was very glad I had brought my wild "youth group" to the screening. When Billy came up front after the movie, he smiled at the whole lot of them. Of course, they were completely freaked out to see this man who had been on the screen just a few moments before now standing in front of them and talking about Jesus Christ. It was a very special night I'll never forget, and I'm guessing those boys won't either.

—Ray Fowler

THREE

IN THE EYE OF THE STORM

IN THE EYE OF THE STORM

"The decision you make tonight

"I thank you for coming tonight. The decisions you make tonight will affect your whole future. And your eternal future, one thousand years from tonight, will depend in large extent on what you decide tonight."

—BILLY GRAHAM

The crowd in the stadium breathed a collective sigh of relief as clouds rolled in and blocked the blistering rays of the sun. Temperatures had already pushed past ninety degrees, and the effects of the heat had become evident on everyone. Sweat-soaked shirts, sunburned faces, parched mouths. Waves of scorching heat had each person longing for some shade.

Seventy-five thousand people had set aside their busy schedules and gathered in a stadium that typically hosted sporting events. But they weren't there to watch football or baseball. They had traveled from near and far to attend to matters of heart and

soul. Tens of thousands of individuals had all been drawn to those stadium seats that day for the same reason—they wanted to know more about God.

As the afternoon passed, the once-welcome clouds thickened and began to darken. Distant thunder was soon accompanied by gusting wind and cool air. A summer thunderstorm was advancing.

Many in the crowd began to pray. If God could part the Red Sea, couldn't He also part the dark rain clouds that were headed for the stadium? The thousands of people there that day, so eager to hear more from Billy Graham, believed He could.

Miraculously, as the attendees' prayers rose from the stadium, the clouds broke into two distinct masses and seemed to split in half, drifting and blowing *around* the stadium. Rain drenched the area surrounding the stadium and lightning flashed nearby, rattling the arena with thunder, but the stadium itself was surrounded by an island of dry land just a few blocks wide. And because of that pocket of calm amid the storm,

thousands of souls were able to hear about the Living Water for the first time.

Welcome to an outdoor Billy Graham evangelistic crusade. Over the years, the crusades have experienced all possible types of distractions and difficulties—storms, intense heat, traffic jams, technical difficulties. But the need of the people never changed.

And Graham and his team have never taken the crowds for granted. They know too well that many forces and pressures beyond their control are at work at any given moment. Poor weather conditions, competing sporting events, and language barriers are just a few of the issues that have often discouraged people from attending and hearing God's good news, the gospel.

Billy Graham greeted crowds by saying, "I know you faced many problems getting here today. But in the name of Christ, I thank you for coming."

When people come to a crusade, Billy Graham welcomes them as if he were inviting a visitor into his home, ushering that person to the most comfortable chair in his living room and making him or her feel like his special guest. He has always reminded members of the crowd as to why they are there that day.

Over the years, Billy Graham has greeted crowds by saying, "I know you faced many problems getting here today. But in the name of Christ, I thank you for coming." And he always wanted to be sure that everyone—no matter what race, creed, or color—received the same welcome embrace.

TAKE DOWN THE ROPES

AS AN ITINERANT PREACHER, Billy Graham has personally spoken to more people than any other individual in history—over 210 million during the course of his ministry. He has preached in churches, synagogues, streets, parks, schools, and every sort of stadium and arena imaginable.

But what is it about Billy Graham that draws so many people to come and hear him? Superficial reasons abound. Graham is one of the most well-known and celebrated men of this century, and many are drawn for that reason alone. But the heartbeat behind people's reasons for coming is the same—the Spirit of God draws individuals to hear this preacher who cares so deeply for them, who wants to point them to Christ.

Graham's great love for people revealed an important truth to him early in his ministry—the importance of making each attendee understand that we are all on equal ground before God. And sometimes that truth must be communicated through action.

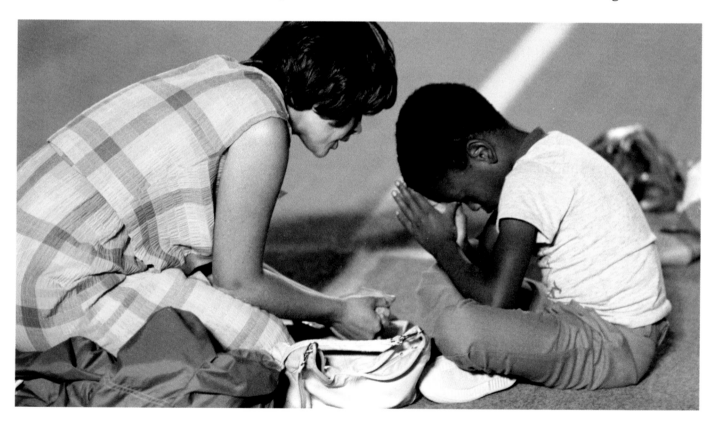

The Spirit of God draws individuals to hear this preacher who cares so deeply for them, who wants to point them to Christ.

The Mississippi of the 1950s was filled with racial tension. Jim Crow laws had enforced "separate but equal" policies that perpetuated economic, educational, and social disadvantages for blacks. Sadly, most people accepted the status quo and the social barriers that kept blacks and whites isolated from one another without giving it a second thought.

In 1952, Billy Graham was preparing for a crusade in Jackson, Mississippi. He looked out at the seating arrangements at the stadium where he would be speaking and discovered something troubling—ropes dividing the seating between whites and blacks. He did not believe that God's people should be segregated for *any* reason. "The ground at the foot of the Cross is level," Graham has said, "and it touches my heart when I see whites standing shoulder to shoulder with blacks at the Cross."

Anger burned inside Graham when he first noticed the ropes that would separate the whites and blacks who attended the crusade. And he couldn't stand by silently and allow God's people to be segregated in the one place where they should be united. So Graham quickly gathered some influential people, and at great physical and financial risk, together they permanently dismantled and removed the ropes.

Bill was only twelve years old when he attended the crusade in Jackson that year and saw Graham and the others tearing down the ropes. He has never forgotten the image of the young preacher urging others to get rid of those symbols of segregation and discrimination.

"The ground at the foot of the Cross is level," Graham has said, "and it touches my heart when I see whites standing shoulder to shoulder with blacks at the Cross."

At the time, Bill's father was a leader at his church in Jackson and one of the most successful businessmen in the area. He was also one of the volunteers who helped Graham remove the racial barriers that late afternoon in Jackson. And Bill's father suffered as a result of his brave actions. Some of his friends' attitudes toward him cooled in the weeks and months following his actions at the crusade. His business began to lose sales as well. He was even soundly defeated when he ran for a city commissioner position a few years later.

A half century later, Bill is still proud of his father's courageous actions in 1952. He speaks of the public rejection his father suffered, but he remembers his father's dignity and courage in standing up to the ridicule and gossip. "My dad never knew how many lives would be affected just by taking down those ropes," Bill says. Some, like his father, paid a heavy price for standing up for their convictions at that crusade. And as a result others, like many black members of the community, had the opportunity to hear and experience the gospel in ways that made God's love more real and more authentic than ever before.

Many around the world have hungered for the same opportunities. And Billy Graham responded to their pleas.

ALL PEOPLE IN ALL PLACES

THE DEEP SOUTH OF THE 1950s wasn't the only area facing difficulties for people who wanted to hear God's message to humankind. Communism, a political straightjacket demanding conformity, hovered like a poisonous cloud over Eastern Europe. One of communism's stated objectives was to "free" people from what was called the "superstitious belief in religion." But no political doctrine could quell the spiritual hunger of millions who thirsted for a relationship with God.

Over the years, Billy Graham repeatedly found himself stepping into that dark and gloomy part of the globe. He was often allowed to visit countries whose governments were actively persecuting Christians. Amazingly, unlikely doors opened for Billy Graham, doors that seemed to invite, if not demand, him to enter. One such place was Romania in September 1985.

Tina was a teenager living in Bucharest the year the Billy Graham team arrived. Along with many others Romanians, she quickly realized how unusual and extraordinary this visit was. When the Graham organization arrived, they were overwhelmed by the welcome they received from the people of Romania. Almost everywhere they went, thousands of citizens gathered, hoping to catch a glimpse of the famous messenger. Tina had traveled to the largest Pentecostal church in Bucharest with the hope of hearing Billy Graham in person, a hope that was realized that cool September afternoon.

From his earliest days…Billy Graham's focus has remained sharp—
all people in all places need to know the living God.

Decades later, her memory of that event is sharp. "Just seconds before he walked in, along with pastors and priests from all denominations, the combined choir and orchestra started to play and sing. They turned on many, many lights in the church. At the moment when Mr. Graham got on the podium, I felt like the rapture was occurring!"

Everyone in that church sanctuary shared Tina's sense of ecstatic joy. "I will never forget that day," Tina says, "that unforgettable moment in my life. His sermon was simple—not complicated but very powerful. I feel honored and blessed that God allowed me to be part of that unique time in our country's history."

From his earliest days of tearing down the ropes that separated people by skin color to later efforts to break through the Iron Curtain, Billy Graham's focus has remained sharp—*all people in all places need to know the living God.* That is what has kept him continually traveling throughout the world, circling the globe, during his extensive ministry. Sometimes he even found himself ministering in locations that seemed like strange stages from which to tell people about the love of God.

Karen remembers one such place.

FREIGHT FOR THE LORD

IN THE LATE 1950S, KAREN WORKED at McClellan Air Force Base in California. One day, as she was at her desk typing, Karen received an order stating that anyone who wanted to could leave work and go outside to hear Billy Graham speak. Like most of the other office workers, Karen was more than happy to take a break from the clatter of typewriters and the shuffling of paperwork.

Along with a group of workers, Karen headed out the front door of the building. "There he stood, on the freight dock, as people assembled." The memory of that day is clear in Karen's mind. "The power of God accompanied the words Billy spoke that day. Though it's been nearly sixty years now, I'll never forget that great godly man standing on a freight dock and delivering the same message he's always delivered: God loves you, and He'll change your life if you invite Jesus into your heart."

Under beating sun and in the middle of their workday, many people responded at that unlikely pulpit. That day a place where heavy loads of military freight were handled was transformed into a place where emotional and spiritual burdens were forever lifted and removed from the hearts of many.

Throughout his ministry, Billy Graham has been guided by the simple truth that every individual, young and old, stands before God and is accountable to Him. So wherever people are in their life journey, Graham knows it is never too late—or too early—to meet Jesus.

LET THE CHILDREN COME

PEOPLE REMEMBER THEIR FIRSTS. Their first day of school. Their first kiss. Their first car. And especially their first meeting with Jesus Christ. These moments are forever etched into a person's memory and can be recalled decades later with unbelievable clarity.

Lynn remembers the first time she attended a Billy Graham crusade—she was just three years old. "My mother and father took me to the local fairgrounds near our town in Oklahoma to hear a preacher they had seen on our small black-and-white television. I was so little at the time, and yet I still remember watching with amazement as people came from all directions, following one another inside the grandstands.

"They seemed so happy!" she recalls. "People streamed in with Bibles in their hands and smiles on their faces. Even to me, a toddler, it seemed that night was really exciting for everyone." Lynn also remembers that night for another reason—the snow cone her parents allowed her to eat. "Snow cones were served that night, and I was so excited my mom had decided to take me down to the concession area to buy one." A three-year-old with a sweet treat? A seemingly perfect evening...until disaster struck.

All these years later, Lynn hasn't forgotten what happened next. "On our way back to our seats, I dropped my snow cone down the back of this lady's dress." Lynn's mother was horrified, fearing that the evening might be ruined because of Lynn's accident. "My mother was upset, but the lady was so sweet and never missed a beat. She just brushed it off and

"When Billy Graham got up to speak, his voice was full of love for our Lord Jesus Christ, full of love for the people he was talking to."

continued singing along with 'What a Friend We Have in Jesus.'"

As it turned out, the disappointment of losing her snack didn't spoil the evening for Lynn. "When Billy Graham got up to speak, his voice was full of love for our Lord Jesus Christ, full of love for the people he was talking to. I remember that night so well because I could *feel* the happiness and love all around me."

That love drew many people to faith that night, including a little girl with sticky fingers. "I discovered that Jesus loves me—even if I did spill my snow cone down that lady's back," Lynn says. "Billy Graham told me so that night."

But Lynn wasn't the only little one whose life was transformed by Billy Graham. Mary Jane was nine years old when she first heard Billy Graham at Expo '72 in Texas. After hearing him speak, an inspired Mary Jane went home and wrote a poem that she still enjoys reciting:

Preaching a sermon, Billy Graham
And singing a hymn were Jesus Christ's fans
Listening to the sermon, never bored,
And then one jumps up and shouts,
"Praise the Lord!"

And like Mary Jane, Johnna remembers a special afternoon when she was a child, growing up in a small town in Tennessee. She had decided to forgo playing with her friends to stay inside and watch something unusual happening at a football stadium on TV. "I remember sitting in front of the television and staring at the huge football stadium full of people. But the playing field looked a lot different than what I was used to. No players in uniforms, no cheerleaders, no coaches, no scoreboards."

The scene was puzzling for Johnna. "Yet I was drawn to continue watching the activity among the sea of people at the stadium. My friends were outside playing games, but not me. This game was much more appealing."

Johnna had come across a Billy Graham crusade, and God had nudged her to keep watching, even as a child. The more she watched, the more young Johnna found herself enjoying and even participating in the event. "I realized I was listening to singing that grabbed my heart. I had gone to church with my mom regularly, but the singing at church wasn't quite like what I was hearing from the television. I began to sing along and actually learned the hymn 'Just as I Am' while watching the crusade."

God lovingly welcomed little Johnna, a curious little girl who decided to stay inside one afternoon and turn on the television at the very right moment, a moment she remembers with much joy to this day.

"When I join the heavenly choir, I will sing 'Just as I Am' with the highest praise. Thank you, Billy Graham, for being there all those years ago."

Jesus once told His disciples, who were trying to keep children away from him, "Let the little children come to me, and do not hinder them" (Matthew 19:14). Billy Graham has followed that instruction throughout his ministry. And millions, like Lynn, Mary Jane, and Johnna are so grateful he did.

"NOW THAT YOU'RE HERE"

FOR MORE THAN FIFTY YEARS, people have come to hear Billy Graham speak for reasons and motivations that even they haven't always understood. Whatever the reason, when lost, hurting, or even angry people turned up the dial and listened to that radio broadcast or wandered into a crusade that didn't quite make sense or sat down in front of something on television that seemed intriguing, Billy Graham has been there with a message of God's love. It didn't matter *why* people were listening; it only mattered that they *were* listening.

Graham has never judged the motivation behind an open ear and an open heart.

When he began to speak at an event, Billy Graham would often look into the faces of those who had gathered to hear him and feel a mixture of awe and gratitude. These people were here for good news—for *the* good news. After a silent prayer for strength and wisdom, he would say, "Now that you're here…let me tell you about the greatest force for good the world has ever known. Let me tell you about God's love."

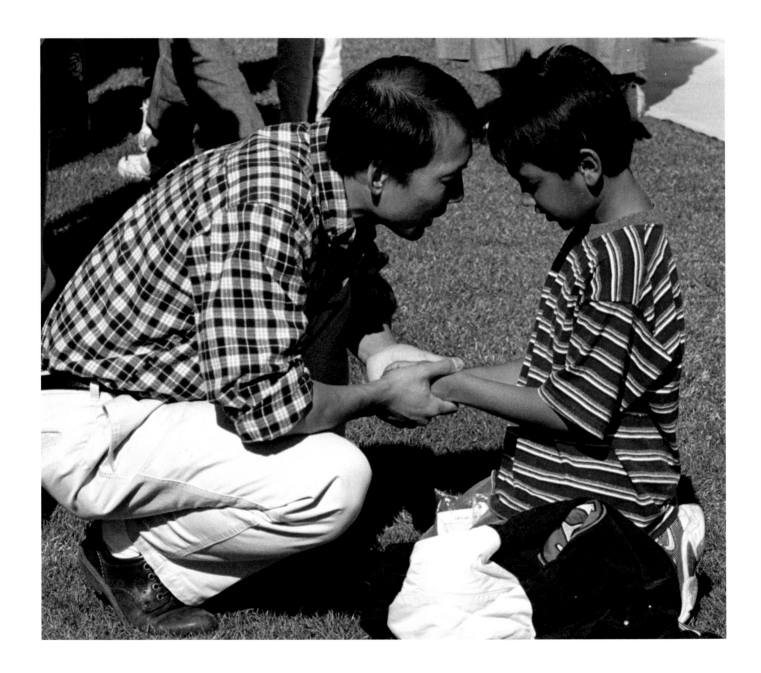

Billy Up Close

I was twelve years old when Billy Graham came to Pittsburgh, Pennsylvania, in 1952. My mother had convinced our little church in Cambridge Springs to charter a bus and attend one of the meetings. We all boarded the bus and traveled over a hundred miles to Pirates Stadium where the services were to be held.

Our group arrived early, found our seats, and noticed Billy and the team checking out the stadium from the infield. As I watched Billy and his team exiting through the dugout right below us, I excitedly asked my mom if I could try to get his autograph. She approved and I bounded over the fence. But they were already in the dugout tunnel, headed back up underneath the stands.

I followed and called out to Dr. Graham from quite a distance. "Billy, may I have your autograph?" He immediately turned and came back toward me. He met me halfway and very humbly gave me his autograph. At the time you'd have thought I had just received an autograph from Mickey Mantle.

Years later, after watching this wonderful servant of the Lord rise to prominence, I now realize how amazing it was that a person of his stature would take time for a kid like me—it's how Christ must've acted when the "least of these" came to see Him.

Thank you, Billy Graham.

—David Mead

FOUR

WITHOUT ONE PLEA

"You can come to Him

"Jesus loves you and you can

come to Him just as you are."

—BILLY GRAHAM

The words of Charlotte Elliott's most famous hymn are familiar to people from all walks of life and in nearly every country around the world:

Just as I am, without one plea,
But that Thy blood was shed for me,
And that Thou bidd'st me come to Thee,
O Lamb of God, I come, I come.

For more than fifty years, Billy Graham has closed each crusade with this simple hymn of invitation, an urging to come

just as you are."

forward to accept Jesus Christ as Lord and Savior. It has been sung in dozens of languages—German, Swedish, Spanish, Japanese, Mandarin, Swahili, and English to name a few.

Just as I am. What a comfort!

The message of the gospel is that Jesus does the saving and spends a lifetime transforming those He has saved.

People are invited to give their lives to Christ—without having to clean themselves up first. The message of the gospel is that Jesus does the saving and spends a lifetime transforming those He has saved.

Thousands of people have walked the aisle at a Billy Graham crusade and prayed to invite Jesus into their hearts. They have come forward alone, holding the hand of a spouse, or shoulder to shoulder with a friend. But the decision is always personal—a plea to be saved through the death and resurrection of Jesus Christ.

Graham's voice has rung out from pulpits around the world, declaring a power-filled message: "Jesus loves you and you can come to Him just as you are." Scores have responded, and many lives have been forever changed—men, women, and children who became children of the Most High God.

Victor is one of those people who was encouraged and comforted by that familiar voice.

Graham's driving passion has always been to communicate the good news to a lost world.

UNIQUE VOICE, SINGLE MESSAGE

"THROUGHOUT MY LIFE, it was the voice that always got me."

Victor, from Minnesota, has been drawn to the voice of Billy Graham for several decades. "No matter where I find myself, if that voice is on the television or radio, I am compelled to stop and listen. The message is so simple, so clear, so compelling that it draws me back to all that matters—my relationship with Christ and where I will spend eternity. I must stop everything and listen because Billy Graham speaks about 'one who has authority.'"

Victor has worked in the field of child protection for many years and has witnessed realities that have often left him despairing over the darkness of the human heart. "I have seen and served children who are beaten, burned, bound, bludgeoned, assaulted, and murdered." Victor's occupation, combined with the ordinary sadness we all face, has on many occasions left a hole in his heart and an unbearable ache in his soul.

"And yet in my darkest hours," he says, "as if God planned it, I have mysteriously come across that voice while sitting in my hotel room flipping through the television channels or in my car, turning the radio dial. Every time I hear Billy Graham's voice, I sense a far greater presence."

Billy Graham knows that the presence Victor and others have often felt is Jesus. His driving passion has always been to communicate the good news to a lost world—the good news that "God so loved the world that he gave his one and only Son, that whoever believes in him shall not perish but have eternal life" (John 3:16). From his early days of preaching in country churches and open-air tents to speaking in stadiums crowded with tens of thousands, Graham has remained focused on that one essential message: *God loves you.*

Allison heard that message—finally. She wasn't ready to listen—*really* listen—for the longest time. Broken, hopeless, and ready to end it all, she "accidentally" stepped on a television remote… and everything changed.

FROM WORTHLESS TO WORTHWHILE

WORTHLESS. Was that really her name? Allison didn't know these days. Maybe it was. That's what her family always called her. She couldn't remember a time when she had felt loved—just the way she was—as a child or as an adult. The constant barrage of criticism from her parents had taken its toll, seeming to smother all hope of love or happiness. Over the years the light in her eyes had grown dim, her expression blank, losing the sparkle every child should have.

"My parents continually told me I was a loser and was useless despite my near flawless grades and outwardly perfect existence," Allison says. "All I longed for was love, friendship, acceptance, and a sense that I mattered in this world."

Although Allison's family belonged to a church, regular participation wasn't important. Allison was taught that God was some type of celestial truancy officer who would "get her" if she didn't behave appropriately. "Other than weddings and funerals, I never attended church while growing up. I wasn't taught about God or His love or salvation or anything of that nature—other than the punishment I would receive if I continued "to be bad."

Is it any surprise that Allison grew up without a sense of self-worth?

Even in her twenties Allison found that she never could live up to her family's expectations.

She eventually got into trouble and had to call home for help, knowing full well she would be ridiculed, and that she was not wanted. "I was the prodigal daughter. My family wasn't interested in welcoming me back home with open arms—just with hate and disapproval and finger-pointing."

"I can't specifically remember every word Billy Graham said, but I do remember the words 'God loves you just as you are, right now.'"

Finally Allison reached the lowest point she'd ever known. She could continue trudging through a world that rejected and condemned her, or she could simply give up. Her choice was to end it all.

"Late one evening I decided that if no one wanted me around and that if there was no real purpose for me here other than to be used, abused, and taken advantage of, then I didn't want any part

of this world," Allison says. "I figured hell couldn't be much worse than what I dealt with on a daily basis."

Allison had reached the end of herself. She felt completely hopeless and useless. "No matter how hard I tried, I was never good enough for anyone. With tears in my eyes, I got up off of my parents' couch with a plan. I was going to drive off a bridge, and I knew no one would even notice I was gone."

But God intervened in a remarkable way. "As I got up from the couch, I stepped on the television remote, and it turned to a channel that was airing a Billy Graham crusade."

Even in her hopelessness and desperation, Allison was drawn to the images and voice coming from the flickering screen. "I can't specifically remember every word Billy Graham said, but I do remember the words 'God loves you just as you are, right now.'

"And I thought, *No. No one loves me.* As he talked with such conviction about love, hope, and forgiveness, I wondered if any of what he was saying could be true. *If this man is willing to share this message with all these people, maybe God has a purpose for me too.*"

Allison finally understood, for the first time, that she was worthwhile to God. That He cared for and valued her. And she gratefully surrendered her life to Him.

"I have found an unexplainable measure of joy, peace, and forgiveness. And most of all I've discovered that I *do* matter in this world and that God has a plan for me, His daughter, and has a seat prepared for me in His eternal kingdom."

Like Allison, many people around the world need time to fully embrace God's message to mankind. Others, such as Melinda, accept the gospel early in life.

A BEAUTIFUL INTRODUCTION

MELINDA GREW UP IN TEXAS. When she was small, her mother took her and her siblings to church, but Melinda's father didn't go with them. "Daddy was a weekend farmer, so his excuse was that he had to stay home to keep things caught up at our small farm. He didn't really like the church rituals either, but always told me he believed in God."

After a Sunday morning of solitude, Melinda's father welcomed an afternoon with his family. "Usually on Sundays after church, we'd all sit down for a nice dinner, and afterward Daddy would turn on the TV to watch a football game. On one particular Sunday, the TV announcer introduced Billy Graham. Momma said she'd like to watch him, and Daddy agreed with only a small grumble.

"I sat on the couch next to my daddy" Melinda recalls. "We listened to the simple but powerful message Brother Graham shared, quoting from John 3:16: 'For God so loved the world that he gave his one and only Son, that whoever believes in him shall not perish but have eternal life.'"

Melinda's family sat quietly in front of the television, absorbing every word. "As always, Brother Graham offered an invitation at the end of his sermon. At that moment, I glanced over at my daddy. Tears were welling up in his eyes and streaming down his cheeks. My daddy believed, and as soon as I realized it, I wanted to be in my Father's house with my family too."

That day, an entire family's future was set on a different course. A dad gained a new understanding of God and His awesome love, and a little girl witnessed her earthly father's introduction to his heavenly Father. The message of love Billy Graham preached brought about the transformation.

Like Melinda's family, some have been changed through a television broadcast of a crusade when they heard Graham deliver the hope of the gospel. Others have received the good news while listening to Graham on the radio or reading one of his many books. A high-school graduate named Elizabeth was one such recipient.

That day, an entire family's future was set on a different course. The message of love Billy Graham preached brought about the transformation.

RECONNECTED

ELIZABETH HAD JUST GRADUATED from high school and was both excited and frightened about entering the new world of college. "I was apprehensive about the unknown challenges and temptations I would face in that environment so far from home. These uncertainties put me on a path to resolve my long-held—and mostly unvoiced—doubts and misgivings about my faith."

Elizabeth needed answers. "Watching and listening to Billy Graham telecasts and radio broadcasts throughout my growing-up years had convicted me about my disconnectedness from God." But something was missing for Elizabeth—an answer that had eluded her to this point.

"As I read the book, the power of the words impacted me in a new way. I was compelled to cry out to God in honest desperation about my lostness."

Elizabeth spent the summer after graduation working to save money for college. One day, while riding in a car with her supervisor, she spotted a package with a return mailing label that read "Billy Graham Evangelistic Association." Inside she found one of Billy Graham's books, *World Aflame*, and began curiously thumbing through it. She was a voracious reader and always eager to find a new page-turner. When her supervisor offered to lend her the book, she immediately accepted.

"And what a godsend that book was!" Elizabeth says. "I had always wondered why I had been so privileged to be born in the Bible Belt of the United States and hear the gospel all my life. In *World Aflame*, Dr. Graham reiterated Jesus's words: 'I am the way and the truth and the life. No one comes to the Father except through me' (John 14:6). I had known this passage since childhood. But as I read the book, the power of the words impacted me in a new way. I was compelled to cry out to God in honest desperation about my lostness.

"No more 'If I'm not saved, save me,' which I had silently uttered in the past when I'd received guidance about salvation. There in my bedroom that night, as I read Billy Graham's book, Christ met me, revealing Himself as my loving and welcoming Savior, putting an end to my anguish and infusing me immediately with His peace. Best of all, this assurance has never faded."

Elizabeth received God's message of love—through the voice of Billy Graham on the pages of a book, a place where you might expect to find inspiration. But people don't often go to a movie theater anticipating a life-changing experience. Diane, however, was one of many who heard Graham communicate the good news as she sat in a local movie theater.

RUNNING TOWARD HOME

"IN 1973 TICKETS WERE AVAILABLE at my church to see a Billy Graham film called *Time to Run*. I didn't know what to expect, but I took a carload of seekers. The family in the film was experiencing conflicts in their relationships. I could really relate to that. One young girl in the film knew and loved Jesus, and I wanted what she had. My heart was open that night."

Near the conclusion of the film, Billy Graham gave an invitation to accept Jesus. Something inside

Diane urged her to go forward, but she was afraid that people would laugh at her.

"My heart was pounding. *Should I go?*" she wondered. *What would my sister-in-law think if I got out of my seat and went forward?*

Diane couldn't deny the pull of the Spirit. "I decided I was going anyway. Amazingly, when I got to the front of the theater, I discovered that my sister-in-law had also accepted the invitation! People were there to pray with us and give us materials about the gospel and the Christian life. Later that evening, after the movie, I read the little book they had given me that talked about God's holiness and my sinfulness. My sin separates me from God. But Jesus closed the gap on the cross and made the way for me to embrace a holy God. I entrusted my life to Jesus that night, and He accepted me just as I was. All the weight of that sin was lifted off my shoulders, and I had amazing peace."

God seeks out people in unlikely situations and places. It's not always a church or a revival meeting.

God will meet people where they are. Christoph, who grew up in East Germany during a time of religious repression, knows this firsthand.

CRUMBLING WALLS

"I HEARD BILLY GRAHAM'S MESSAGE in March 1990 while standing in front of the Berlin Reichstag, the historic German parliament building just steps away from where the Berlin Wall used to divide East and West Germany," Christoph says. "It was a cloudy day, but that didn't stop about a hundred thousand people from gathering."

Christoph grew up behind the Iron Curtain and had been taught that faith in God was foolish, that there was no higher principle of goodness in this world.

"I had observed the fruit of such an empty philosophy while growing up, and all I could see was brokenness and uncertainty. Afraid of becoming like the people around me, of giving in to that hollow belief, I felt a strong longing for hope, for light, and liberty in God. This longing led me to secretly attend church as a young teenager. Since churchgoing was politically incorrect and could have cost me my future, I had to keep it hidden from my family, friends, and teachers."

But just as Christoph was beginning to catch a glimpse of life's ultimate purpose, he suffered a major setback.

Five long years later, when the Berlin Wall came down, Christoph was truly ready to give his heart to Christ.

"I had just opened my mind and heart to the reality of Christ when we discovered that the pastor who had preached to us young people was actually an informant for the Stasi, the official secret police of Germany. He had abused our trust. Deeply disappointed, I turned away from all matters related to God. From that point forward, I was under Stasi surveillance. Not only did that discourage me from searching for God, but it also caused many setbacks in my school career."

Five long years later, when the Berlin Wall came down, Christoph was truly ready to give his heart to Christ. "The wall in my heart crumbled as well. I met Jesus for the first time," Christoph says.

"I was eighteen years old at the time and had started to make my dreams come true. I was working as a junior reporter at a Berlin newspaper, hoping

to become a writer. But my heart was not at peace," Christoph says. "That's why I went to hear Pastor Graham speak. To be honest, I can't remember his exact words. It was more the man than the message that got me. The deep conviction, clarity, and love in his words convinced me that this man knew the Source of what I was looking for.

"As I listened to Billy Graham, I realized for the very first time that *Jesus* was the one calling me, the one who had put that restless longing in my heart since childhood."

Christoph, now a husband and father, lives in New York these days. "By God's grace I have been able to extend His love to others through various works of ministry and in my work as a screenwriter for film and television. I have seen people healed and lives turned around. I will always thank Billy Graham for being a true man of God and for planting the seed that led to my liberation."

"O LAMB OF GOD, I COME…"

A GREAT NUMBER OF PEOPLE have heard the unmistakable voice of Billy Graham, have heard him speak about the incredible love of God—a love that calls people who are weary and burdened to come to Him for rest, a love that calls people to come just as they are.

Billy Graham has consistently preached that God loves *you,* loves every man, woman, and child. And He will receive anyone who surrenders their life to Him. The hymn writer expressed this so beautifully in the final verse of "Just as I Am":

Just as I am, Thou wilt receive,
Will welcome, pardon, cleanse, relieve;
Because Thy promise I believe,
O Lamb of God, I come, I come!

Multitudes all over the world have sung those words, made their way to the altar, and received pardon, cleansing, and relief from Christ—and all because a preacher from the foothills of North Carolina remained faithful to his calling to proclaim the gospel of Jesus Christ.

Come as you are, and be prepared for what Jesus will do.

Billy Up Close

I was a flight attendant for many years. On my drive to the airport before work, I typically spent the time praying. One morning I prayed, "Lord, of all the people in the entire world, would You please put Billy Graham on my flight?"

Within three weeks of my request, God answered my prayer. That month I was working a flight that went to Atlanta and then on to Los Angeles. Mr. Graham boarded the flight in Atlanta and took his seat—right where I was assigned to work during that flight. Nothing is impossible with God!

Always the gentleman, Mr. Graham was extremely humble and friendly. There was such kindness and compassion in his eyes, and it was an honor for me to serve him. He touched my heart, and I have never forgotten that day. I thank God for that divine appointment and for allowing me to meet a great man with such genuine humility.

Thank you, Billy Graham. I saw Jesus in you firsthand!

—Maurilla Sewares

FIVE

THE CRUCIAL MOMENT OF DECISION

"*The buses will wait.*"

"Come to Christ now.

Don't worry about being

left behind. Come now.

The buses will wait."

—BILLY GRAHAM

A choir sang and a preacher stood at the front of a five-thousand-seat makeshift auditorium, urging people to give their lives to Jesus. A lanky sixteen-year-old sat near the front, struggling with an eternal decision. As the final verse of the song rang out, this young man who had once referred to religion as "hogwash" found himself walking down the aisle, surrendering his life to Jesus Christ. The year was 1934. The young man was Billy Graham.

Because of his own experience, Billy Graham knows that in those crucial moments of spiritual decision, some people simply

need a little more time. Sometimes pride gets in the way. Sometimes people are afraid of what others will think. Sometimes it's something as simple as hoping that the buses that brought you to the crusade will wait for you.

But the decision is the same. And Billy Graham's words have never changed: "Come to Christ now. Don't worry about being left behind. Come now. The buses will wait." That simple phrase has opened the door for many people to respond to and embrace the living God.

*In those crucial moments
of spiritual decision,
[Billy Graham knows that]
some people simply need a
little more time.*

SHE DIDN'T SHOW UP...BUT GOD DID

ELIZABETH WAS THRILLED ABOUT the opportunity to hear Billy Graham speak in Sacramento in 1995. She became even more excited when her sister agreed to go with her. "I prayed for months before the event that my sister would be so moved by the powerful message of Jesus's love that she would accept Him on that glorious day!" Upon arriving at the crusade, Elizabeth's excitement quickly turned to disappointment. "My sister wasn't there. I searched the stands near where she should be but couldn't see her anywhere. Discouraged, I took my seat among my friends from church."

Though Elizabeth had been trained as a crusade counselor, that night she was in no mood to talk with people who came forward. Where was her sister? "I was angry with God. How could He let this happen? I had been praying and praying, and I knew I was praying according to God's will. He would want her saved, and yet my sister didn't show up.

"The lower level of the arena was filled with thousands of people who had responded to God's call on their hearts through His humble servant Billy Graham."

"I was really upset and wasn't in the right frame of mind to counsel others. As I sat there, I bowed my head and wept. I told God how disappointed I was and how badly I wanted my sister to accept Jesus as her Lord and Savior. After I cried my heart out to God, He whispered gently to my spirit, 'Look up. These are your sisters and brothers!' And when I lifted my head, I saw that the lower level of the arena was filled with thousands of people who had responded to God's call on their hearts through His humble servant Billy Graham."

Though her sister hadn't come, God did not disappoint Elizabeth... Many, many others had joined the family of God that night!

"My heart swelled as I realized the miracles that were unfolding before me. I rose from my seat and, with tears streaming down my face, made my way into the crowd. As I descended the stairs, I asked God to forgive me and to help me minister to others that night. I found a family that needed someone to pray with them as they sought God's forgiveness for their sins and asked Jesus Christ to be their Lord and Savior. I welcomed them into the family with great joy!"

God showed up that night in Sacramento and introduced Elizabeth to many new brothers and sisters. Numerous others have been blessed with a similar experience. Judy and her sister both responded to God's invitation on the very same night.

LOST AND FOUND

ON A HOT SUMMER EVENING IN 1956, a teenage Judy and her older sister sat with relatives at the Oklahoma City fairgrounds waiting to hear a young preacher named Billy Graham. "My sis and I had attended church all our lives and were 'good little girls' growing up. But that night, as I listened to this fiery preacher, I heard with spiritual ears some things I'd never grasped before."

Judy understood for the first time that she was separated from God and why Jesus had to die for her. "One of the verses stuck in my head: 'What will it profit a man if he gains the whole world and forfeits his soul?' (Matthew 16:26). From my naive perspective, I believed I had pretty much gained the world already, but what Billy shared made complete sense in my mind and heart. I didn't want to lose my soul—I wanted God."

Judy longed to make a decision for Christ that night but was hesitant about responding to the invitation. "When the choir started singing 'Just as I Am,' I ached to go forward. But we were high in the bleachers, and a long line of relatives and strangers stood between me and the aisle. I chickened out. Deeply troubled, I confided in my sister later that night. 'I really wanted to go forward tonight,' I said. My sis, who has always been there for me, told me she would take me back the next evening so I could follow through with my desire. And she did.

For many, making a choice to follow Christ can be terrifying. Billy Graham has always urged people to surrender their fears and doubts and make a public profession.

"The next night I listened intently, knowing exactly what I wanted and needed to do when the time came."

Judy wasn't prepared for what happened next. "To my surprise, when 'Just as I Am' began, my sister hopped up from her seat and started down the aisle ahead of me. I followed, unsure of her motives until we met at the foot of the stage where Billy stood. She looked at me and said, 'I need to do this too!'"

The two sisters were ushered into the counseling tent—and into the family of God. "Billy came into the tent shortly afterward, and those who had received Christ walked by one by one and shook his hand. When my turn came, I remember his piercing blue eyes looking into mine. 'Did you receive Christ as your Savior tonight?' he asked me. 'Do you want to live for Jesus?'

"I said yes and I meant it," Judy notes. "And I've been saying yes to the Lord for over fifty years now as He has led me through valleys and onto mountaintops."

One question recurs to Judy: "What if I hadn't gone back to hear Billy the second night? I never could've made it through these years without Christ."

For many, making a choice to follow Christ can be terrifying. Billy Graham has always urged people

to surrender their fears and doubts and make a public profession. Melissa found herself wrestling with those very emotions when she heard an invitation from Billy Graham.

"STAND UP AND LIVE FOR ME"

ON MOTHER'S DAY 1976, Billy Graham was preaching at the new Kingdome in Seattle,

Washington. Melissa had decided that she couldn't refuse the offer to see Graham.

"My dear friend Kathy had come to Jesus and kept pestering me to go to the Billy Graham crusade at the Kingdome. I didn't want to go, but Johnny Cash would be performing. I figured I could see the Kingdome, get my Jesus freak friend off my back, and see Johnny Cash—and since it was Mother's Day, I had some leverage with my husband to take me.

After what I had heard in
Billy's sermon, I knew that…
I really wanted Christ in my life.
I wanted Jesus's peace, love,
and forgiveness.

"When I was younger, my family expected that I would become a nun. But through the sixties and seventies I found myself drifting further from my faith. Oh, I still believed in Jesus, especially during emergencies and on Christmas and Easter."

"So there I was at Billy's crusade. The Kingdome was three thousand people over capacity, so there was no altar call. After the sermon, Billy asked us to stand up if we wanted Jesus in our life. After what I had heard in Billy's sermon, I knew that I had to stand. I wanted Jesus's peace, love, and forgiveness. I had no idea what would happen to me if I stood and acknowledged that I really wanted Christ in my life."

Melissa struggled to rise up out of her seat. "Billy kept asking, and I kept sitting there, bargaining with God—this wasn't my style, all this emotion and preaching. 'I can't do this, God,' I said. 'I promise to start going back to church and to read the Bible more often. Anything but this oversimplified act of

standing up for You.' But God kept saying, 'Stand up. Surrender your pride and all you think you know about Me and stand up and live for Me.'

"I felt as if two heavy weights on my shoulders were holding me in the chair. A mysterious struggle between good and evil was going on. I summoned all my strength and stood," Melissa remembers. "I let God back in. Of course, He had never left me, I had left Him. He had never stopped calling me to Himself."

Melissa knew she needed to set aside her pride and allow her heart to open up in order for God to truly enter. "Since that difficult, grace-filled moment at a Billy Graham crusade, which I went to for all the wrong reasons, my life was changed, grace upon grace, mercy upon mercy, forever and ever eternally."

Herb was another person who wrestled with this weighty decision. As he watched a televised crusade on a cold winter night, he was brought to the point of surrender.

> *"My life was changed, grace upon grace, mercy upon mercy, forever and ever eternally."*

HE SAID YES

MORE THAN THIRTY YEARS have passed since his uncle Herb's unmistakable transformation, and Ron is still moved. "In 1965, my uncle Herb was home watching one of Billy Graham's crusades on TV while his wife was at church. Although Herb wanted nothing to do with God, he listened to the message. When his wife got

home, she could see that something was bothering Herb. She asked him what was wrong, and he told her about Graham's message and that the Spirit of God had convicted him of his sins. She asked if he wanted to give his heart to the Lord, and he eagerly said yes. From that moment on, Uncle Herb's life changed."

Herb's transformation caught the attention of people around him. "Everyone who knew Herb was amazed. Just by looking at him you could tell that something had happened. Everywhere he went, he told people about Jesus. Almost two years later, my uncle Herb, his wife, and their adopted baby boy were killed in a car accident. Herb's life and death impacted so many people. He and many others are in heaven today because of Dr. Graham and his wonderful message."

The ripple effect caused by Billy Graham's presentation of God's Word often passed from parent to child and from friend to friend. A life transformed by Christ has the power to transform others.

Bill, from New Hampshire, experienced a dramatic change in his life. Though he had never even heard of Billy Graham, he encountered someone who had and that made all the difference in the world.

LIFE OR DEATH IN NEW YORK

BILL'S GROWING-UP YEARS WERE marred by tragedy and bad choices. "In 1968, my father died in a hail of bullets as he attempted to rob a bank. I was only sixteen at the time. The oldest of four boys, I led all my brothers into drug abuse and crime." It wasn't a promising start for a teenager, who seemed destined to follow in his father's footsteps, until God changed Bill's story.

"I got saved in 1981 as a result of a group of Christians conducting a street meeting in Yonkers, New York." The leader of the group, Mike DeCarmine, shared the good news with Bill that day.

Mike had been saved in New York City twenty-five years earlier after listening to a young evangelist named Billy Graham. Bill recalls Mike's testimony:

"In 1957, at Madison Square Garden, while Billy Graham gave the invitation, Mike knelt in the sawdust under the bleachers and trusted Christ."

That decision led Mike DeCarmine to the streets of Yonkers, which ultimately led him to a troubled teen named Bill. That day on the street, Bill was embraced by his heavenly Father, who would never disappoint or lead him astray. "I believe my coming to Christ has a direct link to Billy Graham and the ministry God entrusted to him. I don't know if he'll see this story personally, but whether he does or not, I know I'll see him in paradise."

Other teens have also discovered this life in Christ through the message proclaimed by Billy Graham. But few conversions seemed more unlikely then when God got the attention of a group of rowdy teens.

TEENAGERS TRANSFORMED

MORGAN AND HIS WIFE HAD the worst seats in the stadium. "We were sitting in the nosebleed section, surrounded by a sea of unruly teens.

"We were amid the power of God...and I saw Him move. Thank you, Billy, for being faithful to your call."

The hundreds of churches represented had brought teens. You know how teenagers can be—lots of talking and passing notes and disrupting the service.

When Billy started to preach, Morgan and his wife were distracted by all the commotion around them. But suddenly, about halfway through the sermon, a hush fell over the entire group.

What Morgan remembers most is the response of the teens around them. "Weeping, lots of weeping," he says. "All around us teens were weeping. Then just before the invitation a lot more were weeping and dozens got up and walked down the stairs—before the invitation had even been given. Hundreds left their seats to go forward to receive Christ that evening. It had a tremendous impact on my wife and me. That was the only time we've seen Billy in person, but I look at the crusades in a different way now."

Thousands of lives, including hundreds of teenagers were changed that night. Morgan and his wife felt the impact as well. "We were amid the power of God that night and saw Him move. Thank you, Billy, for being faithful to your call."

In light of eternity, it's never too late (or too early) to change course. David, a pastor in Florida, shares the story of a member of his church who couldn't help but tell everyone about how God saved him—at the tender age of sixty-five.

NEVER TOO LATE...OR TOO EARLY

IN 1973, WHEN I WAS TWENTY-FIVE, I assumed the pastorate of a church in Panama City, Florida. I quickly met Lottie and Earl, an elderly couple who were the delight of the church.

"The first time I talked with Earl, he told me how he had come to faith in Christ—at the age of sixty-five while watching a Billy Graham televison special. He showed me the exact spot in his living room where he prayed to receive Jesus as Billy led the prayer. Over the next four years, I heard Earl tell that story scores of times. Each time, he told it with the same conviction and enthusiasm as the first time.

"Earl was a great encouragement to me as a young pastor. When I had a tough day, I'd visit Earl, knowing that somewhere in the conversation he would again tell me about watching Billy Graham on TV and how it changed his life forever. He said that when he got to heaven, he wanted to see Jesus and Billy Graham."

As Earl learned, it's never too late to accept God's invitation. And it can also happen to those who are just getting started.

Marnie and Jim went to a Billy Graham crusade in Denver in 1987. They took their three-year-old son, Jon, along, hoping he would sit quietly without distracting others. The one thing they never imagined was that such a young heart would respond to God's call.

"We deeply appreciated the music, testimonies, and message given that day," Marnie recalls. "At the end of the day, Rev. Graham gave the invitation to accept Jesus. My husband and I were already believers, so we prepared to leave. Suddenly Jon said he wanted to go down front. He wanted to receive Jesus too. So my husband carried him to the front, and three-year-old Jon received Jesus that day."

Jon's story testifies to the words of Jesus: "Let the little children come to me and do not hinder them, for the kingdom of God belongs to such as these" (Mark 10:14). In many instances, God has used Billy Graham to bring parents and children to Himself at different times. Betty Jean and her daughter are one such family.

FROM GENERATION TO GENERATION

BETTY JEAN GREW UP IN THE CHURCH. As a teenager she prayed often, trying to make sense of her life. "I married right out of high school, and my husband and I attended a large church."

But their spiritual lives were empty. "Praying took place only during a major problem or a family emergency. I would put my Bible away if I heard my husband because I felt embarrassed and that he wouldn't approve of me." And Betty Jean was always irritated when Billy Graham was on TV.

"The televised crusades preempted my favorite programs! One night I came home from the neighbors', and my husband was watching a crusade on TV.

"'What are you watching that for?' I said.

"To my surprise, he pointed at the TV and said, 'This guy makes a lot of sense.'

"*Yeah, sure!* I thought. He changed channels shortly after that."

Betty Jean can't remember if it was that month or the next, but she turned on the TV and Billy Graham was preaching again. Instead of getting irritated, this time she chose to listen. "I had never heard of asking Jesus into my heart and life," she says. "Billy said that you may have been a Sunday School teacher or gone to church all of your life, but have you ever had a personal relationship with Jesus."

Betty Jean realized this described her. "The next day I decided to get on my knees. *Lord,* I prayed. *I already believe that You died for me, but I didn't know I needed to ask You into my heart and life. Please come in. I give You my life.*"

She never had an emotion-filled conversion experience, but from that day on, Betty Jean noticed a change in what she valued and how she looked at life and her choices. "Jesus was changing me," she says.

These were not the only plans God had for Betty Jean and her family. "When my daughter was fifteen, I talked with her about giving her heart to Jesus."

Only God could have orchestrated and sustained the life…of such a faithful servant…named Billy Graham.

But Betty Jean's daughter wasn't interested. "I believe, but I'll do that after I'm grown. Otherwise I might not have fun now as a teenager," she said.

Her resistance weighed heavy on Betty Jean's heart. "A couple evenings later, I was watching Billy Graham on TV, and she was in the living room with me. I got a call and left the room. When I returned some time later, I discovered that my daughter had just prayed with Billy Graham to receive Jesus into her heart. What a blessing that both my daughter and I came to Christ through the ministry of Billy Graham!"

Betty Jean and her daughter learned that God will pursue us until we surrender to His loving and eternal embrace. They laid aside their distractions, heard the call of the Holy Spirit, and responded to God's call delivered through the voice of Billy Graham.

A NEW HEART, A NEW LIFE

OVER THE YEARS, Billy Graham has offered the same simple invitation:

I'm going to ask you to get out of your seat and come and stand quietly and reverently as an indication that you're receiving Christ, that you want a new heart and a new life from this moment on, that you're going to change the direction of your life. The Holy Spirit has been speaking. He's been preparing your heart.

Now you come and receive Christ. If you're with friends or relatives, they'll wait on you. I am not going to keep you long. But I am asking you to come and stand here and say by coming, "I give my life to Christ. I want a new life. I want a new heart. I want forgiveness of my past. I want Christ in my life and in my heart."

And for decades, people have continued to come forward, filling the aisles, surrounding the podium, standing in empty living rooms, pulling their cars over on the side of the road, kneeling next to their beds, and praying on street corners. The location does not matter, but the surrender of one's heart to God does.

Hundreds of thousands of lives have been eternally changed because of one man's simple obedience.

Only God could have orchestrated and sustained the life and ministry of such a faithful servant—a servant named Billy Graham. The time for salvation is *now*—your spiritual needs deserve immediate attention.

Your friends and family will wait.
The housework and bills and your job will wait.
The buses will wait.
Come to Christ now.

Billy Up Close

My mother is the oldest child of Billy and Ruth Graham, and I am the youngest of seven children and the sixteenth grandchild. We have always called our grandfather, "Daddy Bill."

Perhaps Daddy Bill's greatest impact on my life has been his authentic humility. He truly believes he is just a typical country preacher. He has told me on many occasions, "I am not a great preacher, Antony, and you know I don't claim to be. I've heard great preachers many times and wished I were one of them. I am just an ordinary man communicating the gospel the best way I know how."

My grandfather has accomplished more than most of us will in a lifetime, and he seriously believes he is just a regular man. The Bible verse that always comes to mind when I think of Daddy Bill is "to slander no one, to be peaceable and considerate, and to show true humility toward all men" (Titus 3:2, NIV).

As I have grown older and spent more time with Daddy Bill, I've been blessed to witness this humility in a variety of settings. I can remember a time when my grandfather was in south Florida for a board meeting and was feeling somewhat lonely. He took out his personal phone book and began to look for friends who lived in the area. He found the names of a couple he had met years earlier and decided to call and invite them for dinner at the hotel. I'll never forget him saying, "Hello? Hey, how are you? This is Billy. Billy Graham. Do you remember me?" I couldn't believe a man who has been listed by *Time* magazine as one of the most respected men of the twentieth century truly thought this couple could have forgotten who he was!

My grandfather continues to remind me what the journey of life is all about, and for that I will be eternally grateful. Thank you, Daddy Bill, for being the most loving and wonderful grandfather anyone could wish for.

I love you with all my heart.

—Antony Tchividjian

SIX

SEE WHAT HE WILL DO

"You are not just saved from something...

"God loves you and

has a plan for your life."

—BILLY GRAHAM

After each invitation, at the end of every message, Billy Graham crosses his arms, bows his head, and prays for all those who will come forward and accept Jesus Christ. He knows that the people who surrender their lives to Christ are at the beginning of a lifelong adventure—a personal relationship with God. And He has a purpose for each of His children, a life that is more than a random series of events.

Graham has often said, "You are not just saved *from* something—sin and its consequences—you are also saved *for* something—to serve and honor God. You see, God has a plan for your life."

you are also saved for something."

After people leave the stadiums, turn off their television sets or radios, or close the books they were reading, they are at the dawn of a never-ending journey with God.

"Wouldn't it be wonderful to go home tonight, lay your head on the pillow, and know that all the past is forgiven?" he asks. "What a relief! What a load lifted! But more than that, what a relief to know that the Holy Spirit lives within you—to give you strength for tomorrow and to add a new dimension to your life, to offer power and joy and peace like you've never known.

> *"Wouldn't it be wonderful to go home tonight, lay your head on the pillow, and know that all the past is forgiven?"*

"He can change your life," Graham has promised seekers. "It's all yours tonight by giving your life to Christ."

Every story in this book has been a response to that truth. Surrendering to Jesus is only the beginning. God has a plan for people's lives—a plan that always involves pointing others to Jesus.

When Paul looks back, he can see clearly how God used his mother, who was saved at a Billy Graham crusade. The dramatic change in her life spoke volumes to his alcoholic father—and changed his life forever.

A NEW PATH

PAUL'S MOTHER, NANCY, married very young. She had fallen in love with a man who turned out to be an alcoholic, a gambler, and a womanizer. Soon Nancy found herself alone, a working single mother with a one-year-old daughter. She married again, hoping her new husband would be different. Instead, she discovered that he too was preoccupied with gambling and alcohol. This was the family Paul was born into.

Nancy knew her life was falling apart. She longed for something that would hold it all together. And she found it at a Billy Graham crusade in Dallas, Texas.

When Graham gave the invitation, Nancy immediately surrendered her life to Jesus Christ. Paul says of his mother, "Her life took a remarkable new direction. She realized her sins were forgiven and found new life. The change was so dramatic that within a year, her second husband, my father, accepted Christ as well."

Those life-changing decisions set Paul's family on a whole new course—a course with purpose, a course that pointed many to Jesus. "As his Christian faith grew over the following ten years," Paul says, "my father felt the call to become a pastor. When I was eleven, we moved so he could attend seminary, and all of our lives headed in an entirely new direction. Despite pervasive financial hardships and enduring health problems, Mom's "joy light" always shined brightly. The hallmark of her life was the love and grace she extended to everyone. She judged no one and treated strangers as lifelong friends."

Paul remembers his mother bringing soldiers stationed at a nearby army base to their home for Thanksgiving because they had nowhere to go. "When adulterous women were thrown out of their homes, Mom would give them refuge."

> *Billy Graham has devoted his years to traveling the world, sowing the seeds of life in Christ.*

Nancy and her family often encountered people who mocked their transformation and took advantage of their kindness and love. But that made no difference to Nancy. "One stranger Mom took into our home stole her diamond wedding ring, which she had placed on the windowsill above the kitchen sink while she washed dishes.

This man lifted her ring after my mom had fed him breakfast, washed his dirty dishes, and changed his bed linens."

"But even losing her precious ring didn't change her behavior toward strangers. Nothing could steal her joy or her commitment to be like Christ. My mom was the most Christ-like person I've ever known."

Billy Graham has devoted his years to traveling the world, sowing the seeds of life in Christ. Some people might think he wasted his time and wonder if he really made a difference. But Paul knows the truth.

"When I think of the impact Billy Graham had on my mom," Paul says. "I am reminded of the boy

who tried to rescue hundreds of sea turtles that had washed up on the beach during a storm. One at a time, the boy picked up the turtles and carried them back to the water. A man came along and asked what he was doing.

"After the boy explained, the man responded, 'Well, son, you're wasting your time. You won't be able to save all these turtles. And it really doesn't matter anyway.'

"'Well, mister,' the boy said, 'if this turtle was you, I bet it would matter.'"

The connection for Paul is obvious. "At times I'm sure the enormous task Rev. Graham accepted from God seemed impossible, that it wasn't making a difference, that he couldn't reach everyone who needed the good news of Jesus Christ. I want Billy Graham to know that he reached my mom, and it mattered."

It *did* matter to Nancy, to her family, and to the many people who were placed in her path. It mattered to Douglas too. As a result of Graham's ministry, Douglas has spent much of his life serving God in the remotest and poorest parts of the globe.

TO KNOW CHRIST AND MAKE HIM KNOWN

DOUGLAS WAS ONLY SEVEN when he heard Billy Graham speak at a church in the Chicago area in 1948. But the young evangelist's words burned deeply into Douglas's young heart. "Later that same evening, alone in my room, I knelt by my bed and received Jesus into my heart, just as Billy Graham had invited."

Douglas had another strong influence at the time—a Christian doctor who taught his Sunday school class and encouraged Douglas to pursue a medical career.

"My only prayer is that I remain faithful to the high calling of God in Christ Jesus!"

"After college, I headed to medical school at Northwestern. During my last year, in 1965, I served my first short-term mission in Swaziland, Africa, for six months. That experience changed my heart and the direction of my life. During my time there, it became clear that God planned to use me for His kingdom overseas."

God led Douglas to put together a nonprofit organization called Global Medical Education. "In the past thirteen years," Douglas says, "I've taught as a medical educator in sixty-four nations, with a special emphasis on China. God has used me—and thus blessed me—in ways remarkable even to me. My life's aim is to know Christ and make Him known."

As he thinks about his life's journey, Douglas realizes he still has plenty to do. "As I head into my final years with this earthly body, my only prayer is that I remain faithful to the high calling of God in Christ Jesus! I do not intend to 'retire' from kingdom work. I praise God for bringing me to hear Billy Graham almost sixty years ago!"

Like Douglas, John found his life unfolding in unimaginable ways because of hearing the good news that God had a special purpose for his life.

THE YANK WHO SPOKE FOR GOD

ENGLAND WAS A TOUGH PLACE to live during World War II. Goods were rationed, and danger fell from the sky almost daily in the form of bombs and bullets. Once the war had ended, many people were hungry for lasting peace.

John's parents were among those looking for something more than mere survival. Shortly after the war, John's dad learned that Billy Graham was in England. "Let's go hear what this Yank has to say," he told his family, not having any idea how this event would transform their lives.

God's plan for this British family quickly became clear after they responded to the invitation. They moved to the United States and began a new life in Pennsylvania. But God's

ultimate objective involved more than just a change of location.

"A few years later," John says, "Dad felt the Lord calling him to become a pastor. He served the Lord for thirty-five years. Both Dad and Mom are gone now, but through their conversions, many have come to Christ, including my granddad and grandmom; my sister, her husband, and three children; my brother, his wife, and four children; me, my wife, and our three children...I could go on and on. Generations have been touched by the love of the Lord because that 'Yank' listened to the voice of God. Thank you, Billy Graham."

Selma also discovered the ripple effect of Billy Graham's ministry. A student she took to a crusade went on to become a pastor's wife, spreading the truth of the gospel and influencing generations.

TEACHING THE TEACHER

IN 1951, SELMA WAS in her second year of teaching school. That year Billy Graham arrived in Fort Worth, Texas, to hold a crusade. As she looked into her students' faces, Selma knew that God was calling her to take a step of faith. Selma told the students that with their parents' permission, she and her husband would pick them up and take them to the Billy Graham crusade.

God honored Selma's faithfulness, and many of her students were allowed to attend. "We had a full car each of the four Friday nights," Selma says. "At the end of the crusade, all of my students had become Christians! I treasure this experience and am grateful for the positive influence God made upon my students' lives." What happened to those students in 1951 was life changing. Years later, Selma learned how much one life continued to be affected as a result of that crusade.

"My family had moved from Fort Worth," Selma says. "Some years later we went back for a visit. I was picking up my sister-in-law from work. Nita mentioned to one of her coworkers that her sister-in-law, Selma, was picking her up."

> *"Jesus really did make a difference during that Billy Graham crusade."*

Nita's coworker Marcella asked if Selma had ever taught at Bludworth School in Fort Worth. After it was confirmed, Marcella began to share that Selma had been her teacher for two years. Back in 1951, students filled Selma's car the four Friday nights during the Billy Graham crusade. Marcella explained that she was one of the students who had become a Christian during that crusade.

Marcella's husband was now a student at a local theological seminary, and Selma couldn't have been more pleased. "I was encouraged to know that our efforts continued to bear fruit. Jesus really did make a difference during that Billy Graham crusade."

Sometimes it takes several decades to see all that the Lord is doing. That was certainly true for Ellen's parents, who emigrated from Russia to the United States. Many years later, when Ellen's parents were in their seventies, they felt called to reach out to those they had left behind.

BACK TO RUSSIA, WITH LOVE

IN THE 1930s, ELLEN'S PARENTS escaped out of Russia with their respecive families to Iran. Ellen's mother met and married her husband in Tehran and moved to the United States after World War II.

"My Russian mother was a Russian Baptist when she married my father. He wasn't a Christian, but

God's hand was on my father. For as long as I can remember, my father was earnestly seeking God. We were very involved in the Russian community in Los Angeles, and my maternal grandmother and mother persevered in praying for my father's salvation." Their prayers were answered in 1963 when Billy Graham came to the Los Angeles Memorial

Coliseum for a crusade. Ellen recalls, "I was in eighth grade and attended the crusade every night with my father. I'll never forget the night my dad got out of his seat and made the long walk down to the field to acknowledge God's call on his life. What a glorious day!"

It was not only a day of celebration but also a time when lives were forever changed.

"My parents returned to Russia when they were in their seventies," Ellen says, "and started a Bible study and then a church in the village where some of their relatives still live. My father baptized many, and God used him to bring hope and salvation to this little community. Today, at eighty-four, my father is still actively serving the Lord."

God's plans for our lives are often unexpected. But they are always for an eternal purpose. Today there are people in a small Russian village that are eternally grateful that God saved Ellen's father at a Billy Graham crusade in 1963, which brought the good news of the gospel to them many years later.

Cheryl was another who experienced an unexpected cascade of events—events that took her through a deep valley and then back into the arms of her Father.

HOPE IN THE VALLEY

CHERYL HEARD A LOUD KNOCK on her back door, a knock that brought a message no parent wants to receive. Her neighbor was pale and frantic. "She told me about a car accident down the street. My only daughter, sixteen-year-old Sonya, had been killed. It was the worst day of my life."

Amid her deep grief, Cheryl discovered that she wasn't walking this dark and difficult valley alone. Jesus was by her side providing much-needed love and hope. "Through the years I had listened to Billy Graham on television, read his writings, and deeply respected him. But I had never known him like I would get to over the years following Sonya's death. Dr. Graham taught me that it was okay to be honest with God because He already knows my thoughts and feelings."

Because of Billy Graham, Jesus Christ became my best friend. "Twenty years earlier, I had accepted Jesus Christ, but I didn't really know Him until 1980, when I began that difficult journey after Sonya's death. I remember wondering where God was when my daughter died, and I heard the answer—He was in the same place as when His own Son died."

Cheryl's faith was tested over and over as she soaked up Dr. Graham's sermons. "I spent a lot of time dwelling on Billy's messages about salvation and forgiveness. I had to forgive the person who had caused my daughter's death, it was not easy."

"[Billy Graham] is a reflection of the love of Jesus Christ I so desperately need each and every day."

Can good come from tragedy? Hope from despair? Forgiveness from anger? In time, Cheryl learned that the answer is yes—but only through the hope, love, and peace freely given by God. As Cheryl began to emerge from the valley, she found herself wanting to give back to her heavenly Father.

"When I received Sonya's death settlement, I wanted to tithe the money. I asked God to give me the wisdom to know where I should give it. I've never regretted tithing it to the Billy Graham Evangelistic Association. God has richly blessed me just through knowing that my gift was used to promote the gospel of Jesus Christ around the world."

Although they never met, Cheryl feels a deep kinship with Billy Graham. His faithful proclamation of the grace of God was the beacon that guided her through troubled waters. "Dr. Graham is like family to me. He has inspired me to survive a lot of difficult and lonely times in my life. He is a reflection of the love of Jesus Christ I so desperately need each and every day."

Oftentimes God uses others as an example for our Christian walk. Drew is one of many who are grateful for Billy Graham's perseverance in sharing the good news with all who will listen.

"BILLY, YOU INSPIRED ME..."

THE MINISTRY AND WORK of Billy Graham has affected and encouraged people from all walks of life. Some are reached for the first time through the *Billy Graham Classic Crusades* on television. Twenty-one-year-old Drew is one of these.

"As I watched some of Billy Graham's crusades on TV several years ago, I became convicted about my lack of effort in reaching the lost for God. So many simple opportunities to share were available to me, and I didn't use them. Yet here on TV was a man who I believe would do anything to make Christ known, even if it caused great inconvenience. Even if it meant changing his plans in order to serve God, Billy Graham wouldn't hesitate or think twice about it."

*Come as you are...
surrender your life to Christ...
and see what He will do.*

Billy Graham inspired Drew to begin sharing the gospel to whoever will listen. "I now share my faith whenever and wherever I'm able. I don't know if I'll follow in the footsteps of Billy, but I know one thing—I want my entire life from beginning to end to be devoted to nothing less than Jesus Christ! Thank you, Dr. Graham. You have inspired me by your messages, put a smile on my face, and encouraged me to do God's will at all times."

During the more than fifty years of Billy Graham's ministry, millions have heard the truth that God loves them and wants to have a relationship with them. And many have given their lives to Jesus. Those who have accepted the invitation at a crusade, alone in their bedrooms, stopped in the middle of the sidewalk, or anywhere else, continue to impact lives all over the world.

It started with one man, a simple message, and a God with the power to radically change lives.

Come as you are...surrender your life to Christ... and see what He will do.

Billy Up Close

My story starts back when my husband, Tim, and I were trying to have a child. We had struggled with infertility problems for eight years before God blessed us with a baby boy. However, our son, Taylor, was born with medical problems, specifically tracheoesophageal fistula (TEF). His esophagus was not connected to his stomach. If he ate or drank anything, it could aspirate into his lungs.

We were sent to Minneapolis Children's Hospital where Taylor was to undergo surgery. My husband and I were so afraid and kept asking God how after eight years of waiting something could be so wrong. Taylor's surgery went well, but then one morning he got a blood clot in his kidney from having the catheter in too long.

Taylor's body started to shut down, and we weren't sure if he would make it. I remember crying out to God, "Why? Why? Why?" We spent almost every waking moment at the hospital. One day the nurses and a social worker told us we should get out of the hospital for a break, so we decided to go for a walk around Lake Calhoun.

We walked and talked, not really noticing anyone we passed. Then Billy Graham walked by. He was incognito, wearing a Minnesota Twins baseball hat. But as soon as we passed him, my husband and I looked at each other and said, "That was Billy Graham!" It was as if God made us aware at the same moment.

We turned around and ran excitedly toward Dr. Graham. He was such a gentleman as he took off his hat and greeted us. We shared with Billy that we had seen him at a crusade in Fargo, North Dakota. We thanked him for his awesome work for the Lord and told him about our son. He wrote a "Get Well Soon" note to Taylor and signed it, and gave us each a hug before we said our goodbyes. We both felt such peace after talking with Billy Graham. Back at the hospital, we excitedly shared our experience with everyone.

The amazing thing is that the day before our encounter with Billy Graham, my husband told me that if he could meet anyone before he died, he wanted to meet Billy Graham. God works in mysterious ways, and Tim got his wish. Things began to turn around for Taylor as well. Since then, our son has done very well and has never needed another surgery. God restored his health.

We are so grateful for the hope God gave us by sending Billy Graham across our path that sunny day in August 1993.

—Gwen Watson

Invitation

I f the stories in this book caused you to wonder about your own relationship with God, please read on...

The Bible tells us, "for all have sinned and fall short of the glory of God"(Romans 3:23). It goes on to say, "For the wages of sin is death, but the free gift of God is eternal life in Christ Jesus our Lord" (Romans 6:23). Our sins have eternally separated us from our Creator—the perfect and holy God.

Fortunately, that is not the end of the story. With a love that cannot be described or contained, God gave up his one and only Son, Jesus Christ, to pay the penalty for our sin. Scripture says, "For God so loved the world, that he gave His only Son, that whoever believes in Him should not perish but have eternal life. For God did not send his Son into the world to condemn the world, but in order that the world might be saved through him" (John 3:16–17). It is through the sacrificial death and resurrection of Jesus Christ alone that gives us the right to be called children of God.

You may be asking, "What must I do to have a relationship with Jesus Christ?" There is absolutely nothing that anyone can ever do to earn God's acceptance. God accepts you solely through the sacrificial work of Jesus Christ. Scripture states, "For by Grace you have been saved through faith. And this is not your own doing; it is the gift of God" (Ephesians 2:8). Thus, a relationship with God begins when you accept this glorious, free gift through Jesus Christ and surrender your life to Him just like the people you have read about in this book. This will begin an incredible new journey that will ultimately lead you into the presence of our Lord and God.

There is no particular saying or prayer that one must utter in order to accept this God-given gift. However, many find the prayer below to be helpful in putting words to what they feel in their hearts. This is a prayer that Billy Graham would often lead at the conclusion of each "Invitation." And now we invite you to come—to surrender yourself to the living God.

Dear Lord Jesus, I know that I am a sinner and need your forgiveness.
I believe you died for my sins. I want to turn from my sins and turn toward you.
I now invite you to come into my heart and life.
I accept you and want to trust and follow you as Lord and Savior.
In Jesus's name, amen.

If you have surrendered your life to Christ, it is very important

that you begin to read God's word, the Bible, while also

seeking a Christ-loving church and fellowship with other Christians.

For more information that will assist you on this new journey, or simply to

learn more about the Billy Graham Evangelistic Association, please visit

www.bgea.org

If you have a story of how you became a Christian through the ministry

of Billy Graham or want to read the amazing stories of others, please visit

www.thankyoubilly.com

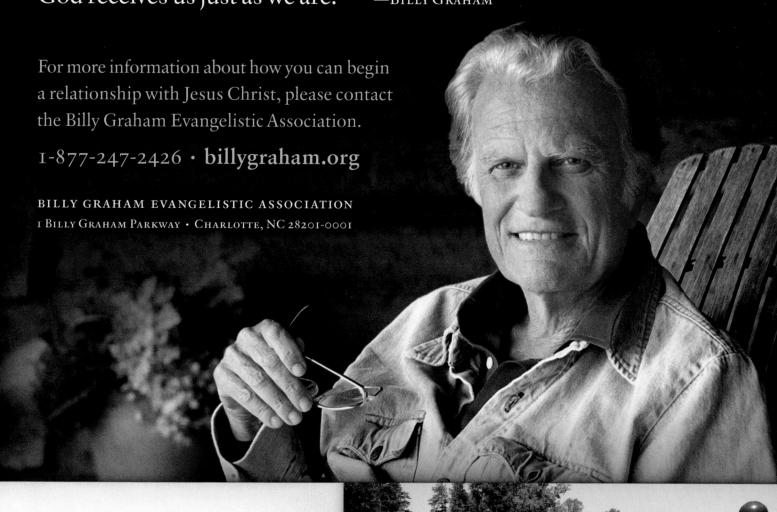